NOSTR

 a beginner's guide

TERESA MOOREY

Hodder & Stoughton

A MEMBER OF THE HODDER HEADLINE GROUP

Orders: please contact Bookpoint Ltd, 39 Milton Park, Abingdon, Oxon OX14 4TD.
Telephone: (44) 01235 827720, Fax: (44) 01235 400454. Lines are open from
9.00–6.00, Monday to Saturday, with a 24-hour message answering service.
Email address: orders@bookpoint.co.uk

British Library Cataloguing in Publication Data
A catalogue record for this title is available from The British Library

ISBN 0 340 77989 6

First published 2000
Impression number 10 9 8 7 6 5 4 3 2 1
Year   2005 2004 2003 2002 2001 2000

Typeset by Transet Limited, Coventry, England.
Printed in Great Britain for Hodder & Stoughton Educational, a division of Hodder
Headline plc, 338 Euston Road, London NW1 3BH by Cox and Wyman Limited,
Reading, Berks.

CONTENTS

INTRODUCTION

Welcome to the strange and wonderful territory of prophecy. This is a world of allegory and image, terrible beasts, fire and deluge. Sometimes it is a glorious place where the trees bear fruit of gold. Walking these lands is perilous, and only the chosen few pass here, usually because they must. One such, it seems, was the prophet, Nostradamus.

Michel de Notredame was the original name of this famous seer, who lived in France in the sixteenth century. He was a doctor and astrologer, seemingly devoted to helping others and no stranger to personal tragedy in his own life. It is believed that he foresaw many historic events of his own and future times, and these have been handed down to us in various writings. In them we can trace many

of the great events of the world, from the death of local kings to the two world wars and possibly to such matters as the AIDS virus. Many of the predictions have yet to be fulfilled and may indicate a third world war, earthquakes, pollution and the advent of a Golden Age after conflict is resolved.

In the following pages we shall be looking at some of the most notable of the quatrains written by Nostradamus and their interpretation. Some appear to be very accurate even to the name of Hitler, which, some say, Nostradamus gave with the alteration of only one letter, almost 400 years before his birth. Is it easy for us to be wise after the event? Surely most of the quatrains could be interpreted in many different ways? And if we are to take prophecy seriously does that mean we are fated, or are we free? This question, one that has teased philosophers for millennia, has special relevance for us in our individualistic modern outlook.

The world of Michel de Notredame was infested with pestilence and scarred by brutality. Our world is apparently different – but maybe not different enough. If any prophet is to have worth, it must surely be to offer guidance. In the chapters of this book we explore what we can learn from Nostradamus.

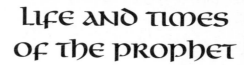

LIFE AND TIMES
OF THE PROPHET

Historian…
Tell our descendants of our hapless fate,
That they may read and weep for our estate,
And let them these their fathers' sins recall
Lest like misfortunes should themselves befall.

Ronsard, *Discours des miséres de ce temps*

It is not sufficient merely to contemplate the words of Nostradamus as if they constitute an oracle issuing from outside the usual bounds of space and time. Nostradamus was a real man, and flawed like every other human, and he was also a product of his time. How he expressed himself, the events upon which he focused and even the way he thought was shaped by the century in which he lived. If we are to come close to understanding some of Nostradamus, or

even to glimpse the reasons why we do not understand, we need to know something about the times that produced him.

We are apt to regard our times as perilous, fraught with the possibility of mass destruction in a variety of ways. It is a fact that we have the means to destroy ourselves utterly as a species, and possibly take the planet with us. However, in the developed world most people, most of the time are comfortable and safe. Even the horrors of our time are a subject for open, global debate. The media, democracy and communications give each of us the illusion, at any rate, that we can direct our lives and have at least some effect on the course of events. In this the gulf between us and the ordinary French man or woman of the sixteenth century could hardly be wider.

FRANCE IN THE SIXTEENTH CENTURY

At this time France was scarcely a nation. Aquitaine and Provence had united only in the previous century, there was still dispute over Calais and other territories claimed by the Holy Roman Emperor, and Brittany was separate until 1547. Local lords exercised considerable power and local traditions held sway, so that royal edicts were often largely ineffectual. The rights and status of the peasantry varied, but were generally worth very little – most aristocrats valued their horses above a village of peasants. In addition, communication was almost non-existent for there was no postal system, only a difficult and expensive network of couriers and the roads were, for the most part, dirt tracks, traversed on horseback alone, not even in horse-drawn carriages. The life of the ordinary person was arduous, painful and usually short, while the lives of the aristocracy were better in some ways, although they carried the ever-present threat of death by intrigue at the hands of one's peers.

Powerful rulers such as Henri II and his wife Catherine de' Medici strove to hold together the straggling kingdom, but they were beset by more than internal dissent. This was the time of the late

Renaissance, when the human spirit flowered in such people as Michelangelo, Erasmus, Rabelais, Raphael and Leonardo da Vinci. Magellan strove to sail around the world and science was advancing while the aristocracy created scenes of unparalleled splendour, such as the historic meeting between Henry VIII and Francis I at the Field of the Cloth of Gold. However, plague was rampant, turning whole towns into open graves and Europe was menaced continually by the Ottoman Turks whose barbaric cruelty and fixation upon conquest obsessed the contemporary European mind. Bands of robbers also rampaged through the countryside.

Religious wars were to claim the lives of more than one and a half million French people before the end of the century. For this was also the era of Calvin and Luther; the new Protestantism was ranging itself against the might of the Inquisition and the Jesuits. If this were not enough the weather worsened in the middle of the century to produce agricultural crises and widespread famine, and the powerful king, Henri II, allowed himself to be killed in a duel, despite the warnings of Nostradamus. Soldiers from disbanded armies joined robbers in the killing and looting, the offspring of Henri and Catherine took it in turns to take the throne and die, and hatred poisoned all, from the highest to the lowest, as Protestant and Catholic lords schemed one against the other.

Nostradamus lived in an age when the Apocalypse seemed close at hand and the Four Horsemen, plague, famine, war and death, scoured the land.

The early Life of Michel de Notredame

Michel de Notredame (or Nostredame) was born at noon on December 14, 1503, in St-Remy-de-Provence. Because of the discrepancies between the Julian calendar and our own Gregorian reckoning, the Sun, which enters Capricorn at the Winter Solstice on or around December 22 in our times, was already in the 2nd degree

of the Cardinal Earth sign at his birth, conjunct (i.e. placed together in the zodiac) both Mercury and the Midheaven, which astrologers will recognise as highly apposite for one who was to become famous through his words. The horoscope of Nostradamus, cast for his birthdate, at Salon, is supplied for interest's sake. However, it should be noted that no true and authentic chart for the seer has been found, and it is one of the mysteries of the life of Nostradamus that, in an era when horoscopes were regularly drawn up for births, none was apparently drawn for him.

His father was a prosperous merchant, Jaume de Notredame, who was himself the son of a Jewish merchant, Guy Gassonet. Guy had converted to Christianity in 1463, taking the name Pierre from the local bishop and de Notredame from the Visitation of Our Lady, on which festival the conversion took place. The family probably originated with the Spanish Jews who had fled persecution in the previous two centuries. Michel's maternal great-grandfather took charge of his education, instructing him in Latin and Greek, astronomy, astrology, medicine, chemistry, herbalism and probably also mathematics. Michel apparently had an irrepressible sense of humour along with an aptitude for learning and an interest in the classics. At the age of 16 he attended college at Avignon to learn rhetoric, logic and grammar, and he became known for his sharp wit. His nickname, prophetically, was *le petit astrologue*. However, the college was disbanded in 1520 when plague stalked eastwards.

For the following nine years Michel became the traditional 'wandering Jew', going from place to place, gathering knowledge about medicinal herbs and plants and their origins. The country was in ferment, threatened by the Turks, the Holy Roman Empire and by plague, and Nostradamus went about treating those who were ill and gathering valuable experience. When he was 25 years old, Michel enrolled for his doctorate at the Montpellier medical faculty, possibly financed by money from his father. Tradition holds that he was elected to the faculty after gaining his doctorate, but there is no record of this, and whatever the case, he was soon on his travels once more, later to set himself up in practice in Agen, in 1533. Here he met a man whose Latinised name was Julius Caesar Scaliger, a true Renaissance character, versed in science, the arts and in

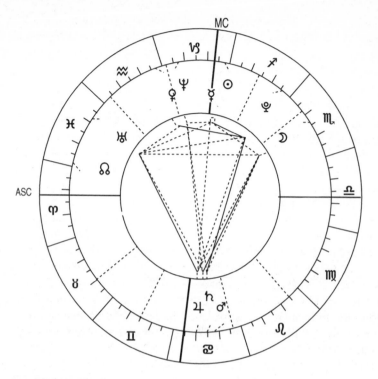

RADIX NOSTRADAMUS
Gmt 12 0 Date 24 12 1503
Lat 43 20 N Long 5 0 E

					Placidus			
☉	♑	1	38	9		2	♉	21
☽	♏	15	56	7		3	♊	15
☿	♑	4	12r	9		11	♑	27
♀	♒	2	23	11		12	♒	26
♂	♋	18	38r	4				
♃	♋	10	56r	4				
♄	♋	15	24r	4				
♅	♓	8	39	12				
♆	♑	22	40	10				
♇	♐	3	40	8				
AS	♈	12	21	1				
MC	♑	6	10	10				
☊	♓	28	41r	12				

The horoscope of Nostradamus.

7

grammar, and they became friends. Michel reputedly also married a woman of considerable beauty, put down roots and had two children.

Tragedy struck, and Michel's family was wiped out by the plague. His reputation was hardly enhanced by his failure to save his own kin, and his dead wife's family sued him, presumably for the return of her dowry. It is said he was also summoned to appear before the Inquisition due to some remarks he made about the making of certain statues of the Blessed Virgin, which smacked of possible Protestant sympathies. Scaliger also fell out with him, as he had done with almost everyone else. No doubt bereft and despairing, Michel de Notredame set off on his travels again. By 1544 he was again back in Provence and treated victims of the plague in Marseille, and then in 1546 he went to Aix-en-Provence for the same purpose, and to Salon. His reputation as a plague doctor was growing and some accounts tell how he was loaded down with gifts, many of which he gave away (possibly because they were impossible to transport). In Salon he met his second wife, the recently widowed and well-off Anne Ponsarde, but they did not settle down because he was called to an outbreak in Lyon where the citizenry cried, 'We want the saviour of Aix', so he might save Lyon as he saved Aix.

On November 11, 1547, at the age of 43, Michel de Notredame married the rich young widow and bought a respectable house in Salon. However, he did not live there immediately, choosing instead to go to Italy. The purpose of this journey may have been different from his earlier wanderings, for he gravitated to places such as Florence where ancient manuscripts had been translated by Renaissance scholars. It seems Nostradamus was keen to develop his talent for prophecy, consulting the works of esotericists such as Marsilio Ficino and his pupil, Pico della Mirandola. Translations were available of Pythagoras, Plato, Hermes Trismegistos and of several magic texts including the famous *Clavicula Salomonis*, or *Key of Solomon*, supposedly passed down from the Biblical king himself and comprising instruction for theurgy, i.e. the summoning of spirits and demi-gods. In search of arcane and occult wisdom, possibly wishing to hone his congenital psychic gifts, Nostradamus also visited Naples, Palermo and possibly Sicily.

NOSTRADAMUS THE SEER

In our own times those who wish to develop their psychic gifts are drawn to the natural world, which frees the intuition, to ancient monuments ripe with the wisdom of the ancients, and to books and like minds, where ideas may be discovered, to stimulate and reveal what is hidden. It is likely that Nostradamus found all of these sources of inspiration on his travels. After three years of exploration, when he was 47, Michel de Notredame returned home to Salon, to his new wife and to the most productive phase of his life.

It was now that he first began to sign himself 'Nostradamus' and to publish his *Almanachs*. These were predictive booklets, rather trivial in content, giving glorified weather forecasts and comments about matters military and political. However, as we have seen, the weather was no small concern in sixteenth-century France, and many thousands perished as the result of a poor harvest in the Little Ice Age. The *Almanachs* sold well, bringing him popularity and money, and gaining him the beginnings of his reputation as a prophet.

Nostradamus, as a physician, was well ahead of his time in appreciating the value of fresh, circulating air and clean running water in preventing and treating the plague. Because of this he invested time and money in constructing a network of canals around Salon. More important, led by signs and portents, he began work on the greatest achievement of his life and the one by which we know him, his body of prophecies designed to foretell the history of the world. Using his intellect, his wealth of experience and learning, he went to work, composing his prophecies into quatrains or four-line verses. He wished to compile ten volumes, each composed of 100 quatrains, and each volume called a *centurie*. This term can be misleading – it was nothing to do with 100-year periods, although bearing in mind the nature of the prophecies this is an understandable mistake.

The *centuries* came into being along with the first of Anne and Nostradamus' children and by the middle of 1554 he was half-way through his first *centurie*. With the help of his literary and philosophical contacts, it was not hard to get his work published,

and the first set of 353 verses went into print in the spring of 1555. Fame was instantaneous, resulting in a royal summons from the Queen, Catherine de' Medici and by July the prophet was riding uncomfortably towards Paris, saddle-sore and wondering if a grisly death awaited him in the twilight of intrigue that surrounded the splendour of the court. No sooner had he arrived in Paris than he was rushed to the eager Queen for private audience and subsequently ensconced in comfortable quarters, where he held many lucrative consultations – he was also, incidentally, laid up by severe gout, due to the good living! His examination of the horoscopes and constitutions of the three little princes left him stricken and the best he could say to the Queen was 'all your sons will be kings'. She did not appear to have detected the doom within this remark and would no doubt have kept him at court with several other occultists whom she had permanently attached. However, the Parisian authorities had begun to investigate the practise of the occult and Nostradamus, who had escaped the Inquisition on more than one previous occasion, decided that discretion was the better part of valour and left Paris without delay.

An interim edition of the *Propheties* was issued following the massive military debacle of St-Quentin, in August 1557, where the Spaniards inflicted huge losses, casting an atmosphere of doom and gloom upon the nation. In the autumn of that year a fourth child, André, was born to Nostradamus and his wife. Their eldest, Madeleine, was now six, Cesar, who was to become his father's greatest exponent was three, and Charles was one. In an age when 55 was considered old, the demands of a young family upon the ageing prophet must have seemed heavy, but all 1,000 of the quatrains were completed by the end of June 1558. However, during this year there were many upheavals and some extremely bitter attacks on Nostradamus himself. One tract, composed in Latin was entitled *La Première Invective du Seigneur Hercules le François, contre Monstradamus* where Hercules described the astrology of Nostradamus as an impious attempt to 'pull God down from the sky by his beard' and put in his place empty fatality. Ignorant personal abuse followed, along with the allegation that his use of astrology amounted to sorcery, playing with the credulity of the readers. (*Source:* Laurent Vidal *Declaration des Abus Ignorances et Seditions*

de Michel Nostradamus, 1558.) Another pamphlet, probably from the same source was called *Le Monstre d'Abus*, which formed a homophonic anagram of the name 'Nostradamus', appearing to ape the techniques of the Green Language, used by the seer (see Chapter 2 for more on the Green Language). Such vituperative and personal attacks were common at the time, but cannot have done much to encourage the prophet. Whether because of this or some dispute between publishers, it seems that some of the verses went astray at this point, and it was not until two years after the death of the seer, in 1568, that the complete work was produced, although even then 58 verses of the seventh century were missing. They remain lost to this day.

By royal appointment

Publishing difficulties notwithstanding, the nation was in a ferment due to the tragic death of King Henri II while jousting. Henri had been a strong and brave, if somewhat unsubtle, monarch and had fairly effectively held together the ramshackle and belligerent group of provinces that existed in sixteenth-century France. Now disaster had fallen and 50 years of strife and instability were to follow. The death of Henri had apparently been foretold both by the Italian astrologer Luca Gaurica, who had told the King to avoid 'all single combat in an enclosed space, especially during his forty-first year, and by Nostradamus. Certainly Queen Catherine and her court were convinced that the death was a fulfilment of Century I, quatrain XXXV:

> *Le lyon jeune le vieux surmontera*
> *En champ bellique par singulier duelle*
> *Dans caige d'or les yeaux luy creuera:*
> *Deux classes une, puis mourir, mort cruel.*

> *The young lion will overcome the old,*
> *in a warlike field, in single combat.*
> *In a cage of gold he will pierce his eyes:*
> *two wounds being one he then dies a cruel death.*

This quatrain in effect made the reputation of Nostradamus. Despite all warnings, the King insisted upon jousting with the Captain of his Scottish Guard, Montgomery. Montgomery was reluctant, being much younger than the King, but there was no way of avoiding the royal challenge. They rode against each other on the third day of the jousting at St Antoine that marked the marriage of Henri's daughter, Elisabeth, to King Philip of Spain (erstwhile husband of the hapless Mary Tudor) and Henri's sister Marguerite to the Duc de Savoie. Both the King and Montgomery had a lion in their coat of arms. During the third bout Montgomery's lance pierced the gilded helmet of the king (*dans caige d'or...*) and entered his face and brain just above the eye. Some reports say there was also a second wound to the throat. Ten days later he died in agony.

This event, although disastrous for France, did much for the credibility and popularity of the seer. Nostradamus continued with his *Almanachs* and with lesser known works on how to treat cases of plague, and on astrology. He was also consulted by many powerful nobles regarding the future and their personal fortune. He was even approached by the canons of Orange regarding the whereabouts of their stolen treasures. However, in an age of paranoia and persecution, individuals such as Nostradamus were never truly safe. Charges of witchcraft were an ever-present possibility, and because he was of Jewish ancestry and generally 'different' he was illogically suspected of being a Protestant. Add to this the threat of arousing the displeasure of a noble client, and one may wonder at the fact that Nostradamus escaped torture and a very nasty end. Possibly the patronage of the widowed Queen, the cunning and unscrupulous Catherine de' Medici, may have protected him. He set to work on his *Sixains* and at the time of their completion in October 1564, Catherine de' Medici arrived in Salon, with her 14-year-old son, King Charles IX. The royal family had come to consult their seer, during their two-year tour designed to unite the troubled kingdom, and arthritic Nostradamus was called upon to pronounce, publicly, the welcoming address.

On this occasion Henri, Prince de Bearn, was also present and legend holds that Nostradamus intuitively realised that here was the future King Henri IV. He drew up his horoscope and managed to be

present when he arose the next morning, in time to assess the moles on his skin and to make a pronouncement about his royal future. In fact, this amounted to treason, spelling as it did the demise of the current dynasty of Valois, and while Henri IV was wont to recount the tale when he did in fact ascend to the throne, no one seems to have paid much heed at this juncture. When the court and its cavalcade was held up at Arles by the flooding waters of the Rhône, Nostradamus was again summoned to attend the royal family, and appointed Councillor and Physician-in-Ordinary to the King. Along with this post came a pension. At this point the seer, now the father of six children by his second wife, could be seen to have achieved success. However, he was already extremely infirm and plagued by severe arthritis which made it almost impossible for him to ride on horseback.

In the year 1566 Nostradamus was dying. In his set of prophecies known as the *Presages*, one prediction reads: 'On returning from the embassy he puts away the King's gift. His friends and family find him, quite dead, near his bed and bench.' He received Extreme Unction on the evening of July 1 and told his assistant, Chavigny, 'You will not see me alive at sunrise.' He was, indeed, found dead on the floor, in the position foretold in the *Presages*, his body hardly cold. He died on July 2, the day sacred to the Visitation of Our Lady (Notre Dame) and was buried with full civic honours in the former Franciscan chapel in Salon. His tombstone was later replaced by another in the west wall of the Chapel of Our Lady – again Notre Dame. Two of his sons lived fairly successful lives, but the third killed a man in a dual and was thus forced to become a friar. His youngest daughter refused to marry, and despite the fact that the others did, only three grandchildren were produced. Two were sons of his daughters and the other a daughter to one of his sons. Thus the name Nostradamus was not passed on to future generations. This may not have mattered to the seer. It is possible that his true, secret allegiance was to the Goddess, and to ancient pagan mystical traditions. The recurrence of the theme of 'Our Lady' may hint at this. The pagan connections of Nostradamus and his allegiance to the mysterious and powerful Guise family is the subject of a dramatic novel by Liz Greene (see Further reading).

STORIES ABOUT THE SEER

Stories naturally cluster around such figures as Nostradamus, reflecting the mystique and charisma of his image. While these may be essentially apocryphal, they portray Nostradamus as we like to see him. One of the most interesting, suggesting the inescapability of Fate, concerns the selection of a pig to be roasted.

NOSTRADAMUS AND THE WRONG PIG

On visiting a friend for dinner, the seer spotted two piglets in the farmyard, one white and one black. He stated that a wolf would eat the white one and that the black one would be served for dinner. Wanting to play a game with his guest and to see if he could prove him wrong, his host ordered that the white one should be killed for their evening meal, and served up by his cook. The cook did as he was told, and the white piglet was duly killed and prepared for the spit, at which point the cook left the carcass unattended in the kitchen for some moments. While he was gone a tame wolf-cub that was being kept on the farm came into the kitchen and made a meal of the piglet. Nothing further was said, and pork was served at the supper table. The host laughed at Nostradamus, telling him that it was, in fact, the white pig they were eating, but the seer insisted that was not the case. To settle the argument the cook was summoned. He had to confess that the white pig had been eaten by a wolf and that he had to kill the black pig for the meal, and that it was the black pig even now on their forks!

This story has a nice twist. However, it was not put into print until a century after the death of the seer, and then anonymously.

NOSTRADAMUS AND THE FUTURE POPE

While on his travels in Italy, near Ancona, Nostradamus met a swineherd (in some versions, a young friar) going by the same road. The seer cast himself down into the mud, before the feet of this

surprised young man, saying that he must kneel before 'His Holiness'. Later, in 1585, the young man, Felice Peretti, did indeed gain the papal crown, becoming Sixtus V.

It is true that Peretti, born in 1521, was a Franciscan friar from the age of 12. As his father was a gardener, he may have been a swineherd for a short time, and he did originate from the region close by Ancona. However, there is no record of Nostradamus having been in Italy before 1548, and none at all of his having been in Ancona. Besides, Peretti was ordained in 1547, and so it is unlikely that he was travelling the highways and byways at this time. But one cannot be sure...

NOSTRADAMUS AND THE MAIDEN

Having an impish sense of humour and a talent for observing humans and seeing through their behaviour, Nostradamus was not slow to pinpoint the real motives and plans of others. One evening, as the ageing seer was enjoying the summer sun, sitting outside his home in Salon, along came his neighbour's pretty young daughter, on her way to the forest to gather firewood. 'Bonjour, fillette', he said, amiably. Some time later she came back with the firewood, looking a little flushed and dishevelled to be greeted by the words: 'Bonjour, petite femme.' She had gathered more than firewood in the woods, it seems!

Spotting this hardly demanded exceptional intuition, and the story may well be true, except that the very same tale is told of Hippocrates.

NOSTRADAMUS AND THE STRAY

During his sojourn in Paris, in 1555, Nostradamus swiftly became famous and was consulted by many nobles. During this time the de Beauveau family sent their page to his lodgings. This young man had recently lost a valued dog that belonged to his masters. Before the seer had even had a chance to answer the door or ask him what he had come for, he called out, quite untruthfully, that he had come

from the King. Through the closed door Nostradamus called: 'Your lost hound is on the road to Orleans!'. Where, as it turned out, it was found.

The story has a better claim to truth than the others because it was reported by Chavigny, assistant to Nostradamus, and published in his *Vie et testament de Nostradamus*.

TECHNIQUES AND TALENTS OF THE SEER

They saw his pale visage
Emerge from the darkness, his hand
On the rock of Ethernity unclasping
The book of brass.

Blake, *The Book of Urizen*, Chapter III

The physician

In many publications, the abilities of the famous Nostradamus as a doctor and healer are mythologised, crediting him with powers that are almost supernatural, along with some very inspired and

enlightened practises as a man ahead of his time. However, this is not fully borne out by the seer's own writings or by his most immediate biographers. Nostradamus was, in fact, educated in the traditional medicine of the time at the medical school at Montpellier, where he enrolled in the autumn of 1529, a year before the novelist and humanist François Rabelais joined. Contemporary medicine was heavily influenced by Aristotle and Galen, both of whom had the backing of the Church, and so could not be questioned for fear of a charge of heresy.

Hippocrates (born c. 460 BCE), the so-called Father of Medicine, after whom the Hippocratic Oath taken by doctors today is named, was also influential. His approach had much in common with what we would now term 'healthy living', placing emphasis on nature's own gifts, such as diet, exercise, fresh air and occupation. His framework, however, was the concept of the four humours: blood, phlegm, yellow bile and black bile, which correspond to the terms sanguine, phlegmatic, choleric and melancholic. These, in turn, equate with the four basic elements of air, water, fire and earth respectively. The idea of the four elements runs through astrology, ancient and modern, and has found its way into psychology through C.G. Jung, the analytical psychologist and erstwhile follower of Freud, as four primary functions of consciousness. In medieval times and before that, it was believed that the entire Universe was composed of these elements (which indeed it is, in a way) and that health in the individual depended upon a balance of the four humours. The holistic, and indeed homeopathic, approach of Hippocrates has much in common with modern alternative medicine. However, it included the use of purgatives, diuretics and some narcotics, and also recommended blood letting, where appropriate. Hippocrates also decreed that every doctor should travel, to gain experience.

Claudius Galenus or Galen was born in 129 CE and, while he embraced much of the work of Hippocrates, his approach was essentially allopathic, as opposed to homeopathic. This means that, in keeping with our mainstream medicine, he treated symptoms with their opposite. As an example, a patient who was vomiting would be given something that discouraged the body from vomiting, rather

than a minute quantity of a substance that might encourage it, as in the homeopathic approach. Galen also believed in the *pneuma* (which means 'breath' in Greek), an unseen substance in the blood that controlled the physical processes. While Nostradamus appeared to have great respect for Galen (he was too much of a pragmatist not to do so!), he also tended towards the empirical approach, i.e. if it works, use it, and never mind the theory! The approach of Aristotle (born 384 BCE) was originally not favoured by the Church, as it was very analytical. This, however, changed in medieval times to the point where Aristotle's experimental findings were elevated almost to religious dogma. Naturally this exerted influence upon Nostradamus and was not conducive to an individualistic approach.

Thus Nostradamus was a product of his time. He may well have harboured revolutionary ideas and a tendency to use what he found effective, regardless of whether it might fly in the face of accepted theory. He may, indeed, have favoured 'natural' remedies and appreciated the benefits of running water and fresh air. However, in this he was no different from several of his contemporaries, such as the noted Paracelsus (c. 1492–1541), the Swiss physician, who laid many of the foundations of modern pharmaceutics, and others. It is possible Nostradamus possessed some preternatural healing ability and/or superior intuition regarding ailments and their cures, but there appears to be little in the way of concrete evidence for this. Nonetheless, the aura of the Mage is cast over this and other areas of the seer's life.

Medical practice

Because of the importance attributed to the four humours, medical diagnosis tended to rest on the observation of the urine as evidence of what was inside the patient. Astrology was also important as the appropriate astrological chart, usually drawn for the time the patient succumbed and took to his or her bed (a 'decumbiture chart'), could reveal the essence of the matter, again with relevance to the humours. Of great importance in times when death was always

around the next corner was prognosis. Astrology was paramount in this and Nostradamus was in his prophetic element. It was also believed that much disease was due to too much blood, no doubt carrying the concentration of unbalanced humours, hence the practise of bleeding was popular. Nostradamus no doubt used these approaches, although his *Traite des fardemens et confitures – Book of cosmetics and conserves*, published in, or just prior to 1555 – indicates that he also used the practical, homely approaches more common to the then despised apothecary than the doctor.

Being of Jewish descent, and remembering that Jews were often blamed for the plague, the involvement of Nostradamus with this disease is hardly surprising. The plague killed people in such quantities and so swiftly that whole communities were ravaged and cities were reduced to repulsive charnel houses. That Nostradamus was considered an exceptional plague doctor is hardly in dispute. In 1546 he was summoned by the citizens to the plague-stricken Aix-en-Provence, seemingly to direct the medical endeavour. This plague had been called the Black Death because of the colour of the skin induced by subcutaneous haemorrhage. Victims also suffered from *charbons* or buboes which were glowing swellings, appearing all over the body, being inevitably fatal if found on the patient's front, but less grave if on the back alone. This disease was infectious even at a distance of five paces, in fact it was believed that one could catch it merely by being looked upon by a plague victim.

Nostradamus taught that the only effective protection was to suck on a rose pill, of his own prescription, which contained such ingredients as cloves, calamus and cypress wood, as well as rose petals and rose juice. He used the pills himself, and did not fall victim to the disease. All other methods he recounts as being utterly ineffectual, including bleeding, which he did, apparently practise, despite statements by many biographers to the contrary. Thus it is a little hard to ascertain why Nostradamus acquired such an impressive reputation as a plague doctor, except that in all probability he insisted on swinging reforms in public hygiene and sanitation, using insights acquired from Hippocrates. While he was greatly valued in his time as a 'plague expert' there is no absolute proof that he was, or did, anything very extraordinary.

The astrology of Nostradamus

Nostradamus is famous principally for his predictions. There are several ways we may imagine that he came to write his cryptic verse. Possibly it was some kind of 'automatic writing'. Possibly he just wrote down whatever came into his head, and because he wrote so much, so obscurely and with so much attendant imagery, some of it, by the law of averages, has to appear to come true. Indeed, there is no proof that this was not the case. However, because of our knowledge of the seer and his time we can be reasonably sure that he used two chief approaches in his predictive work: astrology and scrying/theurgy.

In the time of Nostradamus the position of astrology was somewhat shaky in respect to the Church and Inquisition. Astrology is not the same as magic. In many ways essentially cerebral in its approach, astrology does not necessarily threaten received wisdom. Its workings may be occult, but it does not imply anything wild, instinctual, pagan or allied to personal revelation. With appropriate disclaimers in regard to divine omnipotence and his own personal devotion to the Holy Church – and with a bit of tact and common sense – the astrologer in the time of Nostradamus could remain reasonably safe and even respectable. Nostradamus' books contained the statement that they held 'nothing contrary to the Faith' and his works were never placed on the Catholic Index of banned books. This says something for the pragmatism of the seer!

Much of the approach of Nostrasamus was based on the ancient concept of cycle. Events repeat themselves in the same way that the planets and stars perform their inevitable round, and there exists a correlation between what is above and what is below, in the tradition established by Hermes Trismegistos. All astrology, ancient and modern, is based upon this precept, and while it remains essentially unproven scientifically, there is a certain amount of cool reason in it, bearing in mind the unity and self-referential quality of the Universe. Having accepted that there is a link between our lives

21

and the motions of the heavens, the rest of the exercise is fairly mathematical, resting upon the drawing up of charts and the observation of the positions of the planets. There are many ways of approaching astrology, of using it for prediction and interpretation. It seems that the one most favoured by Nostradamus was that of comparative horoscopy.

Comparative horoscopy rests, as one might expect, on the comparison of one set of planetary positions with another, similar one. If one notes the event that coincided with the initial line-up one may predict another event very like the first one, when the planets resume their positions. Of course, the planets never line up twice in exactly the same way, at least not within a timescale that we could possibly map. However, the match may be close enough to be significant. This may be easier to understand if we consider an actual event. One of the most interesting examples is the parallel between the line-up of planets at the assassination of Julius Caesar, in comparison with those at the time of the assassination of President Kennedy. This is given by Peter Lemesurier in *The Nostradamus Encyclopedia* (see Further reading). There is no space here to explain the astrological meanings in detail, so if you know very little astrology and want to understand the terms more fully, you may like to start with *Astrology: A Beginner's Guide*, by Graham Boston, in this series.

The match is for February 19/20, 44 BCE, with November 23–29, 1963 CE. The events in question actually took place on March 15, 44 BCE, and November 22, 1963 CE, respectively, so the match is not exact, and one might speculate that the 'event' signified was not so much the assassination itself as something allied to it, such as the conspiracy, or events leading up to and surrounding the key occurrence. The match is as follows.

At around 11 am, Mars, Venus, Mercury and the Sun were all in the 10th house and the Moon was in the 12th house, for both events. In the case of Julius Caesar, Pluto was in the 2nd house and with Kennedy, Jupiter was in the 2nd. Jupiter was in the 9th house for Julius Caesar, while Neptune was in the 9th for Kennedy. Other planetary positions are less relevant. For the purpose of this technique, it may not be of prime consideration what interpretation

one might usually place upon such planetary configurations – all that matters is that they are very similar, and coincide with very similar events. In the case of our example the 10th house could certainly be seen as significant, relating to public image and the authority of the state. (Unlike positions in astrological signs, which may be relevant for days/weeks, house position depends on time of day. Thus when several planets are lined up in a single astrological sign, these will be in each of the 12 houses in turn, for an average of two hours each, during the day.)

The technique could be repeated as follows. First, select a dramatic and significant event from history, the time, date and place of which are known. Then find the date or time period nearest to the event when at least four planets seem appropriately placed by sign or house, using traditional associations and meanings. If the fast-moving Moon is included here, the number should be increased to five, and should include one of the superior planets (Mars, Jupiter or Saturn). Modern astrologers using this technique could include the outer planets Uranus, Neptune or Pluto, which were not known in the days of Nostradamus. Now make an exhaustive search of planetary tables, looking for a match. When this is found, note the angular distance of the Sun from the celestial Equator (i.e. its declination) for each event/time and calculate how far the latter event falls to the south, or north, of the original. If a period of several days is involved the figure for the first and the last days should be noted.

Now, refer back to the latitude of the initial event and correct it in accordance with the relative declination of the Sun, to obtain the approximate latitude for the event to come. (In other words, if the difference between the two mean declinations is 4°, then this adjustment must be made to the latitude of the original event, to establish that of the future event, always bearing in mind the difference between north and south.) All the basics being now in place, a prediction can be made, remembering that the planetary line-up may refer to the time either immediately before the event or just after it. Thus, the configuration may take place a month or so before or after the event. The latitude may also vary by a degree or two. (Longitude was not calculated in the time of Nostradamus, but

likely locations might be selected on the basis of similarity of the place of the first event. In addition, Nostradamus could employ the arbitrary assignation of countries and cities to astrological signs, e.g. both England and France were held to be under the sign of Aries.) Now all you need are a map, some general knowledge about world events, some imagination and intuition.

When evaluating the general climate of a time, or developing a clearer picture of the coming event. Nostradamus would also have used some of the traditional astrological interpretations. Mars, for instance, considered by modern astrologers as indicating assertion/aggression in the natal chart, would, in a mundane chart have been an indication of war, violence and possibly plague. Thus a chart drawn for a crucial time, revealing Mars on the horizon, in the sign Scorpio (for which it is the old ruler) and appearing in square aspect to Saturn, the Greater Malefic planet, might well, all things considered, have been seen as heralding misery and mayhem.

Another factor observed by Nostradamus, albeit very indirectly, is the Precession of the Equinoxes, whereby the equinoctial point moves backwards against the background of stars, making a total circuit approximately every 25,800 years. This period may be subdivided and assigned to specific planets. It seems that Nostradamus may have considered the precessional cycle to be somewhat longer than 25,800 years, and divided it into six, assigning each period to a planet or luminary. For instance, the Age of Saturn, set to run from 2255 CE to 2615 CE, was regarded by the seer as a forthcoming Golden Age, in keeping with an earlier personification of Saturn as god of harvests and the cornucopia of nature.

Other predictive methods

Liz Greene, in her fascinating biographical novel about Nostradamus called *The Dreamer of the Vine* (see Further reading), describes the methods developed by the seer in order to divine the future. There are certain astrologers who assert that astrology, if applied correctly and used for the erection of a horary chart (i.e. a chart drawn up for

the moment a question becomes clear, or is posed, which then provides the answer to the question) is enough in itself to predict the future very accurately. As long as the correct rules are observed, then the interpretation is virtually infallible. Such a belief is reassuringly simple. However, there inevitably ensues argument over which rules are really correct. In the event, personal intuition is bound to enter the picture with astrology, as indeed with most things in life, albeit unobserved for the most part. In any case, it seems that Nostradamus did indeed augment his astrological skills, which some have considered debatable in the first place, with the magical and the occult.

In his *Preface à Cesar*, in which he dedicated his prophecies to his eldest son, then a small child, Nostradamus begged the boy never to use occult methods because of the effect they have on the mind, body and soul. Nostradamus burned his magical works but fortunately referred to them elsewhere. In keeping with the times, all manner of abominations such as the cannibalisation of babies and incest were described as part of rituals to raise demons, and in the next breath piously damned by the writer! The two books that seem to have inspired Nostradamus were *De Daemonibus*, by the neo-Platonist, Psellus, and *De Mysteriis Aegyptiorum*, by the philosopher, Lamblichus. He may also have used the famous grimoire of Solomon, the *Clavicula Salomonis*. Here instructions are given for the raising of spirits in order to obtain knowledge from them, usually about the future. (This practice is called theurgy.) Trance states may be induced by fasting and the inhalation of certain herbs, and rituals similar to those practised by the Delphic Oracle. In such a state revelation may be received. It is possible that Nostradamus also undertook much more complex and extensive rituals, using ritual equipment and clothing and employing a range of arcane symbols. If he did all this, it seems he may well have frightened himself, hence the warning to his son.

Whatever methods he did or did not use, it seems he did find some way to obtain clairvoyant knowledge, not only of the general impressions of a forthcoming event, but even, clairaudiently, to hear names. He admitted to using *un mirouer ardant* – a burning mirror, which may be taken as a flame-ringed magical instrument or, more

probably, a simple mirror, concave in shape, which catches and concentrates the rays of the sun. This is akin to the practise of scrying, a well-known prophetic technique where pictures are discerned in a reflective surface such as water in a cauldron or a 'dark mirror'. Alternatively, Nostradamus may have used the term figuratively. Yet another technique Nostradamus may have employed is 'incubation', where an idea or phrase is repeated before going to sleep, and in the morning the dream images and symbols are recorded. In addition, language itself may have been an avenue to revelation, or at least to the formation of an obscure prophecy. Starting with a 'revealed' line the natural laws of rhyming and verse construction could have led to something that sounded portentous, and at times truly impressive. Finally, Nostradamus may have used 'automatic writing' where one holds a pen, often in the left hand and allows words to 'write themselves', possibly under the direction of some spirit agency.

Because of his own writings and the warnings to his son, we can assume that Nostradamus had first-hand knowledge of some demanding and most esoteric rituals. Specifically, he made sure that, first of all, he was in the correct, calm and detached frame of mind, a prerequisite for anything of this nature. Meditation would have helped in this, along with ritual bathing, fasting and possible celibacy. He remained alone, having no interaction with others, even his family. His rituals were carried out after midnight, and resembled the Delphic Oracle in that, having donned a ritual gown he sat on a tripod over a vessel that contained water and gave off fumes that in all probability were, at least mildly, mind altering. Sitting there in a state of prayer and meditation, an altered state of consciousness would almost inevitably have ensued, in which the seer may have received impressions, and images – even seen visions. These methods are very basic, practised in some form by many people today who have an interest in developing their clairvoyant skills, and they rarely fail to produce at least some result. Because of this the methods carry the ring of truth.

The Language of Nostradamus

Commentators have suggested that Nostradamus never intended anyone to understand what he had written until after the event. This is unconvincing to say the least. After all, it is easy, bearing in mind the multitude of events that take place around the globe, to find something in his predictions to fit everything. While it is probably true that Nostradamus was deliberately ambiguous in order to avoid persecution, criticism or being proved wrong, hindsight is a wonderful thing. If we place any credence at all in the prophetic abilities of the Seer of Salon we have to believe that his writings be interpreted before the event he was predicting – at least sometimes!

Opinions on Nostradamus vary enormously, from those who believe he was the greatest prophet of all time, with awesome supernatural abilities, to those who assert that his verses are meaningless, not worth time and attention. Others have stated that he wrote in code, or codes, that he never intended to be properly understood by anyone, and that he was illiterate! While there is much to suggest that Nostradamus was shambolic, he was not an uneducated fool, as his other works demonstrate. One of the problems facing the Nostradamus scholar is the translation of old French, for in the time of Nostradamus there was no such thing as correct spelling. Nostradamus often used the infinitive form of the verb to convey the future tense and his syntax followed Latin, and was influenced greatly by Virgil. French word endings are not specific enough to retain clear meaning if so jumbled.

The use of Latin words was considered desirable in the sixteenth century, as an enrichment to the French language. Of course, words do not translate exactly from one language to another. Hence the use of apt French words in English, e.g. 'chic' which means so much more than 'smart' and 'grande passion', of which, some might say, the English have little concept in the first place! This is a further consideration when interpreting the seer's work. In addition, the punctuation was often wrong or absent. It is certainly not enough to approach the original writings with a pocket French dictionary and

lots of optimism! In fact, there have been several translations and/or misprints that have given absurd or quite erroneous interpretations. For instance, the birth of a two-headed kid in the same year as the initial printing of the *Propheties* has been reported as the birth of a two-headed foal, because translators have mixed up *cheval* which means 'horse' with *chevreau* which means 'kid'. As another example one of the most frightening quatrains, X.LXXII runs as follows:

L'an mil neuf cens nonante neuf sept mois,
De ciel veindra un grand Roy deffraieur
Resusciter le grand Roy d'Angolmois,
Avant apres Mars regner par bon heur.

The year 1999, seventh month,
A great king of terror will come down from the skies
To revive the great king of Angolmois,
Around the time Mars will reign for the good cause.

However, much rests on the position of an apostrophe, for later editions printed *d'effraieur* which does, indeed, translate as 'of fear'. Without the apostrophe, as given in the probably more authentic versions, *deffraieur* means 'defraying', thus a peacemaker and the very opposite of the terrifying visitation we might imagine! We consider this quatrain in a later chapter.

Thus one can appreciate that there are many variations on translations of Nostradamus, and not a few mistakes and misconceptions on the part of authors and researchers. Unless you are skilled in translation, experienced in old French, have a good basic knowledge of Latin and astrology and are willing to go to efforts to obtain the original Nostradamus scripts, you will have to rely largely on the translations of other people. I think it is important to be clear about this, for many claims have been made in regard to the prophecies, some of them quite apocalyptic, and these may be on the basis of translations that are in dispute even among experts. I might also mention at this point that there are several general misconceptions in circulation regarding the prophecies – for instance, it is widely believed that Nostradamus predicted the end of the world, and that he mentioned Hitler by name. One may read 'end of the world' in some lines if one wishes, for doom and gloom always

have a fatal fascination, but he does not make this, or indeed anything, crystal clear. As for this reference to Hitler, it is more likely he was using the old name for the Danube, 'Hister' which was its name in classical times, when it formed the boundary of the Roman Empire. For such reasons it is necessary to bear in mind the importance of the classical heritage to the scholars of the sixteenth century – and to keep an open mind, generally!

The Green Language

It has been asserted by some writers that Nostradamus wrote in code. He himself stated that he purposely used obscure language, which may be regarded as a type of code, or codes, if one wishes. He called his language *scabreux*. Some writers have described a specific code that he used, shared by other occultists, called the Green Language, or the Language of the Birds. This language is rooted in ancient mythology and in initiation into the mysteries, which means that the initiate has an awareness extending to other realms and meanings. The fact that it is called the Language of the Birds refers to the airy realm of intellect and spirit. 'Green' may be an alchemical term, or may derive from French. *La Langue Ouvert* means 'open language' of ordinary mortals. When this is altered by aphesis to *vert*, it becomes the closed language of the initiate. David Ovason, in *The Secrets of Nostradamus* (see Further reading), defines this language as 'a linguistic method of inducing hidden meanings into various words and phrases according to a system of arcane rules'. It seems to me that such a language may indeed reflect the meaning within meaning perceived by the esotericist, the innate perception of reality as relative and many layered, the magic behind words revealed by the cross-associations between them and the mythical heritage which underpins much of our culture. In practice, however, in relation to Nostradamus this language seems akin to *Daily Telegraph* crossword-speak. *Scabreux*, for instance, contains the word *cabre* meaning 'rearing upwards' and generally used of a horse in the sixteenth century. This can be taken to mean that the language used is secretly a thing of the skies, heading upwards to the realm of the birds.

Homophony is another technique of the Green Language, where words sound alike. For instance, *renard* meaning 'fox' sounds similar to 'reign art' which may be taken to mean the skill of kingship. It also relates to the Old High German *reginhart* meaning 'strong in rule'. Thus, *renard* in quatrain VIII.41, may be taken as relating to a foxy, strong ruler, by several avenues of reference.

> *Esleu sera Renard ne sonnant mot,*
> *Faisant le saint public vivant pain d'orge*
> *Tyrannizer apres tant a un coup*
> *Mettant a pied des plus grands sur la gorge.*

> *A fox will be elected without saying a word,*
> *Publicly playing the saint, living on barley-bread*
> *to tyrannise after so powerful a move*
> *Putting his foot on the throats of the greatest.*

This 'fox' may be Premier Paul Reynaud, Robespierre, a future pope, the antichrist himself or Napoleon III. David Ovason (see Further reading) prefers the interpretation of Napoleon III, due to his extreme cunning, the fact that he was indeed elected, that he swore an oath to support democracy even though he was secretly working to become Emperor and that he did finally tyrannise indeed. He was eventually declared responsible for the ruination of France.

To turn to an example involving myth, *L'oeil de la mer* (the eye of the sea), to which reference is made in quatrain IV.15, has been taken to mean periscopes but more probably means 'whirlpool' as the Greek phrase for whirlpool *mati tis thalassas* means 'the eye of the sea'. In the Greek myth, the monster Charybdis lies off the coast of Sicily, swallowing the ocean and creating dire peril for mariners who must find their way between Charybdis and the six-headed sea monster into whom the nymph Scylla was turned by the witch Circe. So the event in this quatrain probably takes place in Sicily, the line *L'oeil de la mer par avare canine* referring to the two monsters. The full verse runs:

> *D'ou pensera faire venir famine*
> *De la viendra le rassasiement*
> *L'oeil de la mer par avare canine*
> *Pour de l'un l'autre donra huille froment.*

Help will come
From whence one will think to bring famine.
The eye of the sea, by the covetousness of a dog,
For the one will give the other wheat-oil

Erika Cheetham (see Further reading) takes the view that this refers to the blockade of Britain in World War II, taking the translation 'The eye of the sea like a covetous dog' and describing this as a wonderful description of U-boats. Off shore drilling rigs have also been suggested. This provides an example of the many variations in possible approaches and interpretations of Nostradamus. It also illustrates that the Green Language, if it is a code, is not based on simple, easy-to-learn principles or on anything consistent, once it is discovered. In truth, the Green Language leaves us in the same place in regard to Nostradamus – his writing is obscure, complex and hard to interpret. (If you wish to make further study of the Green Language, David Ovason's *The Secrets of Nostradamus* makes informative reading (more details in Further reading).)

Dating the prophecies

The prophecies may be dated in a variety of ways. In some the dating is implied in the interpretation, although this presupposes that the interpretation itself is correct. Authors differ greatly in this. Nostradamus could not date his prophecies in too obvious a manner. If he were too good a prophet he might be accused of witchcraft and heresy, if too ineffectual then he would be laughed at. He was damned if he did, damned if he didn't. The compromise upon which he settled seems to have been effective, for it certainly hasn't detracted from his mystique. He dated a select few, and even those were not dated very obviously.

As we have seen, some of the dating is astrological, based on planetary positions, and these may be pinpointed using an ephemeris (planetary table). The co-ordinates given are generally planets in signs and these configurations tend to repeat, although sometimes with vast intervals in between. When checking this out, it

is best to start with the slowest moving planet, i.e. the one furthest from the Sun, and in the time of Nostradamus this would have been Saturn, which spends about 2½ years in each sign. Jupiter spends a year in each sign. During this period the faster moving planets will have a chance to move around the zodiac. Where Nostradamus refers to being 'under' a sign, this will mean that the Sun is in the sign. Mercury and Venus are always very close to the Sun, often in the same sign.

Another form of dating is by apparently openly stating the year, as in the famous quatrain X.LXXII, *L'an mil neuf cens nonante neuf* although this may be based on some biblical starting point. The liturgy of the Church is sometimes used in similar manner.

Verses may also be dated by association with other verses because they share a similar phrase, or phrases, names of places and/or people, and broader themes. Many of the verses appear to have pairs, although these are rarely placed together in the *centuries*. Once one of the pair can be chronologically placed, its fellow can be placed likewise. Here is one possible pairing:

Century I.XXIII

Au moys troisiesme se levant le soleil
Sanglier, Liepard, au champs Mars pour cobatre
Liepard laisse, au ciel extend son oeil
Un Aigle autour de soleil voit s'esbatre.

In the third month at the rising of the sun
The Boar and the Leopard meets to fight on the field of Mars.
The Leopard, exhausted, casts his eye up to the heavens
To see an Eagle striving around the sun

Century I.XXXVIII

Le Sol & l'aigle au victeur paroistront
Response vaine au vaincu l'on asseure:
Par cor ne crys harnois n'arresteront
Vindicte paix par mors si acheve a l'heure.

To the victor will appear the Sun and the Eagle.
The vanquished will be given vain assurances.
Neither bugle nor shouts will stop the soldiers.
Peace is through death, if achieved in time.

These have been related to the Battle of Waterloo, June 18, 1815. The boar is the Prussian Boar, and the Imperial Eagle, a symbol for France. The battle took place three months after the return of Napoleon from Elba. His grenadiers fought until they were wiped out, to one man. Peace could only come through death of Napoleon, whether literally or in terms of his political power. Here we have an example of two good quatrains, although other interpretations have also been made, such as I.XXXVIII being linked to the peace movement.

Reading the oracle

It is tempting to regard the words of the seer rather like tea leaves in the bottom of a tea cup and to read them accordingly. Certainly one can approach them in that way, and with a good degree of intuition a result may be obtained. However, such insights may be dubious and probably far from the meaning Nostradamus intended. A mishmash of guesswork and schoolroom French will probably yield a result that is even worse! Nostradamus' work needs to be approached with some knowledge of his historical time, his education and his personality. For instance, his repeated references to Muslim invasion reflect something that was considered much more of a real threat and national preoccupation in the time of the seer. Much dire prognostication on his part concerning Muslims has not apparently proved correct, to date.

It seems that the esoteric, in almost any form, readily combines itself with confusion, illusion, fudging and downright charlatanism. There are many reasons for this. Our conceptual frameworks, our cherished beliefs and even our language do not combine happily with the occult. Those who are gifted in this area are indeed often confused. Psychic gifts are generally unreliable, and those who possess them are either not taken seriously or derided, or placed on an uncomfortable and unrealistic pedestal. All of these attitudes are in evidence in regard to Nostradamus. The human ego does not stand up well to invasion by collective and mystical imagery, thus

prominent spiritual figures all too often present themselves as semi-divine and get carried away by their own propaganda. It is tempting, in a world where one's natural gifts are not taken seriously, to give nature a helping hand – in other words to indulge in mystification, even in trickery, and to be purposely obscure in order not to be proved wrong, or to be proved right! Nostradamus was in all probability fraudulent, highly skilled at being portentously vague, good at self-promotion, a gifted psychic and a reasonable astrologer. He also needed to make a living, and to survive in a savage and turbulent time. In other words, he was human. What he said needs to be regarded in that light.

Practice developing the seer within

It is probable that psychic gifts are within the reach of us all. Residual parts of the brain, for which there is little known use, may very possibly be repositories of psychic ability that has atrophied, or that is developing. Cases have been put forward supporting the belief that humankind, in ages past, possessed magical powers far in advance of our own. Stan Gooch, in *Cities of Dreams: When Women Ruled the Earth* (Aulis, 1994), describes his theory that we are descended in part from the Neanderthal race, who were extremely magical, having an enlarged cerebellum – the little 'bun' at the back of the head – which probably gave them superior intuitive abilities. Others have suggested that, in the New Age we are evolving towards a greater, global consciousness, and that our psychic powers are becoming more manifest. Whatever the case, it is certainly possible for each of us to develop our own abilities to see beyond the everyday and to begin to predict the future.

How might we begin this? First, it is well known that contact with nature increases natural intuition. Intuition is indeed a very natural function – the 'sixth sense' comes to life more readily in the realm of the instinctual, although darkened rooms and candlelight do have

their place. So if you wish to develop in this way start by taking time out to observe and be part of the rhythms of nature, go out for long walks in parks or the country and notice trees, birds, wild animals, the drift of the clouds, the scent of the grass. Do this for the enjoyment of it – do not look for portents, for if you are looking for formulae you will be allowing the restless intellect to come between you and your instinctual side, that is finding its way out. Notice the changing of the seasons, and how this evokes change within you. For more information you may like to consult *Paganism: A Beginner's Guide* (Moorey and Moorey, Hodder & Stoughton, 1997) in this series or *The Wheel of the Year: Myth and Magic Through the Seasons* (Moorey and Brideson, Hodder & Stoughton, 1997). However, study and radical change of lifestyle are not necessary for developing intuition at a very basic level – that is unless your life has been very frenetic and materialistic. This is simply about tuning in to the would around you and feeling deeply that you are a part of it.

MEDITATION AND VISUALISATION

It will help if you learn to meditate. There are many approaches to this, starting with the light trance state that most of us naturally fall into from time to time, when looking, say, at a patch of sunlight or candle flame, to more complex and deep states where reality is left further behind. Some approaches concentrate on emptying the mind and disassociating from the everyday totally, 'watching' thoughts as they pass through the mind as if they were appearing on a television screen, and then turning the screen off. Others do not place so much emphasis on the emptying of the mind, as on altering its state by focusing on matters other than the immediate day-to-day reality. For instance, one might 'centre down' by drawing one's stray thoughts back inside, concentrating on the inner core. Such an approach might be a prelude to some type of creative visualisation, a 'pathworking' or a shamanic journey.

Pathworking is usually an inner journey where one is talked through the experience by a group leader or a tape recorder. The detail may

be considerable, or very sketchy, to facilitate personal experience, and some esoteric tradition may underpin the material. In the case of a shamanic journey, the experience will be all one's own, and very vivid, although again the framework of one tradition or another will be present in some form. In theory, we can all journey. In practice, some find it very difficult. However, the purpose here is to achieve an altered state of consciousness, in order to 'stretch' the mind, and we can all do that. Other techniques are also available, such as opening the chakras and working with one's aura. All these require lots of study and practice. There are books in this series on shamanism, chakras and related matters. While you may wish to explore some of these, there is no need to follow any specific path or study in order to increase your basic intuitive skills.

However, the simple skill of quieting the mind for ten minutes per day, at least, will serve to make room for other stimuli, and will at least flag up to your consciousness that you are open and ready for something different. After you have done any exercise such as this, however short and unremarkable, please remember to ground yourself thoroughly afterwards, especially if you are a complete beginner. Take several deep breaths, pat yourself all over, touch the ground and finish off by having a bite to eat or drink. Affirm to yourself that you are back in the 'here and now'.

ReLAXATION

First, it is a good idea to learn how to relax, for tension is what forms the principle barrier between ourselves and the vast sea of energy that is the Universe.

Relaxation practise should be undertaken regularly every day, if you are serious about it. Nothing good will be achieved by a couple of two-hour stints at the weekend – which will probably result in UNconscious relaxation rather than the conscious variety! Ten minutes each day, at a time when you are least likely to fall asleep is to be recommended. Start by lying on your bed, because that will signal to your unconscious mind that you really are relaxing, but you may like to move to a comfortable chair as you become better

at it to avoid falling asleep. Become aware of your body and concentrate on relaxing each muscle, either by slowly tensing and relaxing or by imagining your body is powered by busy little men who are all downing tools and walking off, or by any other method you find works. You will need to practice and experiment to find what works for you, learning to be aware of any little tensions that creep in. The general practice of relaxing will be most beneficial to you whatever you decide to do. You may choose to do it as a prelude to meditation/visualisation sessions or before scrying (see later) or similar activity. Before undertaking any psychic activity, relaxation is a 'must'.

Visualisation

When you feel reasonably adept at conscious relaxation, you may like to progress with some simple visualisation exercises. Please remember that if you have never done this sort of thing before, and especially if you have a pressurised lifestyle, you may need several months of regular practice. Visualisation exercises open up the inner landscape. Here we have the realm of the imagination, which means the image-making faculty through which we can access the subtle realms – this is not about self-deception, although what is apprehended cannot be taken literally, especially at first.

So, when you feel you are deeply relaxed, simply imagine that you are sitting in a theatre, and the curtains in front of the stage are slowly opening upon the landscape of another world. This is your first glimpse of Otherworld, the subtle and beautiful realms that interpenetrate the fabric of our own, but are usually not visible. Just sit in the auditorium, observing the landscape. Notice the colour of the sky, the clouds, trees, grass, rocks or any other landmarks. What is the terrain like? What is the weather like? Do you feel welcomed by this place? Are there any animals or people to be seen? And what scents can you make out? Are there flowers, new-mown grass, wood smoke? What about sounds? Do the birds sing, the streams chatter? Can you hear people talking, laughing, singing? Observe this for as long as you feel comfortable, then allow the curtains to close and come back to everyday awareness.

When you have done this a few times, and when you feel comfortable to do so, you may enter the scene. Choose first a protective symbol to take with you. This may be anything that you trust or has symbolic meaning for you – a cross, a flower, even a teddy-bear! Come out of your seat, along the aisle, slowly up the steps to the stage and into Otherworld. Take a deep breath and savour your surroundings anew. You are quite safe, you can 'come back' any time you choose. You are now able to take an inner journey. Doing this within the framework of a tradition gives you psychic protection, but such an approach is outside the scope of this book. This is to be a short and simple journey, and you have your protective symbol with you. Anything or anybody that you meet on inward travels may be challenged with words such as 'If you mean me good then welcome; if harm, begone!'

Walk slowly through the landscape, following a stony path around the foot of a hill. On the top of the hill burns a bonfire, the smell of the smoke is faint and sweet, carrying a hint of mystery. The wind is in your hair, sighing gently through the emerald leaves above you. You find your path is running alongside a silver stream, bubbling over the rocks, pure and translucent. At length the path crosses the stream via a small wooden bridge and disappears into the ground under the hill. The path now bends gently towards the hill, and the bushes thicken around you. Pushing them back you see the path ends in a small cave.

The fragrant breath of the earth rises from the cave. Do you wish to enter? If not, simply retrace your steps. If so, go in, where it is dark and cool. The cave is lit by a low glimmer and precious stones sparkle on the walls. Take the time to look around you. This is a magical place. Notice all the details for they are important to you. There may be something special here for you, a gift or a message. If so, take this with thanks, even if you do not understand the significance. If it is a gift take it with you, when you are ready to make your return journey, which you should do as slowly as you came, back along the path. Notice any changes that have come about since your outward journey. Come back to the place where you started and say farewell. Now step back out, into the theatre auditorium, resume your seat, set down your protective symbol and

come back to everyday awareness when you are ready – do not hurry. Make a note of what you have experienced and be sure to ground yourself in the ways mentioned earlier.

This method may sometimes yield some clear insights. More likely they will be symbolic, and often, especially at first, they will seem to mean very little, if anything. However, the experience should be very pleasant and calming, and will serve to open your inner sight. If at any point you feel frightened, remember that you have your protective symbol with you. Also, please remember that you should not take things too literally – a skull, for instance, does not by any means necessarily mean death! It is more likely to mean some profound change or the receiving of ancestral wisdom. Anything that frightens you is likely to be a projection of something inside you, some inner fear that you have not sorted out, and while you may take this seriously, you should not take it literally. There is nothing to fear but fear itself. Respect, however, is a must, with any psychic undertaking.

As you become more practised you may use this little 'journey' to gain the answer to specific questions. Again, do not take things too literally! For instance, finding a small effigy of a horse in the cave probably does not mean you should risk your last penny on the favourite in the Gold Cup (but then again, it might!).

BELIEF AND TRUST

As we come to develop our psychic and clairvoyant abilities our beliefs and conditioning are likely to become an important issue. Most of us have very little idea how much our expectations and ingrained ideas actually affect our perception to the point where we do not see things if we don't expect them to be there. Even when we de earnestly believe in other realms, other manifestations beyond the everyday, other capabilities of the human mind, that is not the same as *knowing* that they are there. Belief may stem from a wish to believe that is actually undermined by doubt, either that such things really do exist, or, more likely, that we are capable of making contact

with them ourselves. In the time of Nostradamus, it is most unlikely that the average person had the unadulterated materialism that most of us operate within today. However, concepts of individual development and personal power were also undreamed. Fear and superstition were rife and ranged alongside belief in the supernatural and magical powers was a holy terror of the Church, which told everyone what to believe, on pain of death, or worse. Although we are now less readily credulous and although many individuals simply do not believe that anything exists outside everyday reality – including God and the Devil – in many ways we are more free to experience internal revelation. All we have to learn to do is to recognise, and to trust.

Intuition is like an arm or a leg. It strengthens with use and atrophies if left unused. Like a limb that has 'gone to sleep' the sensations of our intuition are not to be fully trusted at first. We cannot trust a leg that has been bent double underneath us to bear our weight if we decide to walk, and we may have to wait for unpleasant tingling sensations to subside and to give the leg time to adapt to what is now required of it. The bent-up leg may send some quite misleading impressions to the brain about the ground on which we are trying to walk and there may even be referred pain in other parts of the body that are actually quite unaffected. In the same way the intuition has fallen into disuse and disrepair, and we certainly cannot trust every little prompting, every little fancy and fantasy that seems to come from outside us and seems to carry glamour and portent. Indeed, intuition often works best upon the mundane and comes upon one not as some highly coloured and often fearful or haunting image but as some straight and ordinary 'bone knowing'.

So, if intuition is so unreliable, how can we ever trust it? The answer here is that you have to, paradoxical as that may sound. We all respond better if we are trusted. Difficult children, who have shown themselves to be anything but trustworthy, blossom if someone does place trust in them, and so learn to trust themselves. In the same way, we have to make the decision to trust our intuition and act upon it. This is quite practical. It is also very dynamic and means that development takes place quite quickly – much more quickly

than if we were just to sit around saying 'I've got a feeling about so-and-so... I wonder if...'. Trust your intuition about who will win the race, or who will phone you tonight, and act upon it, perhaps by placing a bet or risking making a fool of yourself by saying 'Hi, Sam' before the other person has had time to say anything! Of course, you should only take risks where the outcome matters little, and never where something deeply personal is involved, where it might be all too easy to deceive oneself. As you come to make mistakes, and then, at times, find you are right, you will learn to distinguish between unconscious associations (e.g. just because the name of a horse reminds you of wonderful childhood holidays does not mean that it is 'lucky'), fancies and plain wishful thinking in comparison with the real thing. Consult your intuition at every turn – who is it who is ringing you? Who's at the door? What did so-and-so do today? See how often you are right, and make notes about your findings if you wish, in a special notebook, so you may review the process. In time you will come to trust your intuition so well that you simply 'know' when a job application isn't worth filling in, or whether someone fancies you or not. Such things can save you time and aggravation. However, be very careful that you do not follow such hunches before you are ready, with your tried-and-tested intuition.

Different Methods

If we are to believe the myths told about Nostradamus, we see that he did concern himself with the trivial and the everyday, such as horses, pigs and the loss of a girl's virginity. However, Nostradamus made his name with large-scale prophecy. The principles may be similar, but they are not the same. For the personal and the everyday one can pick up clues unconsciously from pheromones and body language, and by listening to the instincts, one may realise that one actually knows much more than one believes. In respect of future events, however, we need more specific clairvoyance. We have several clues as to the methods used by Nostradamus and some of these may be used with comparative ease.

INCUBATION AND DREAMS

It is very common for large-scale disasters such as earthquakes and plane crashes to be presaged by the dreams of ordinary people, who have no connection with the event. The ability to foretell through dreams may be cultivated in the same way advised for developing the general intuition, simply by taking note of one's dreams. Occasionally one has a dream that seems especially memorable, where something more than the usual imagery seems to be involved. Such dreams may indeed mean we have had an out-of-body encounter with someone else while both of us were asleep, or they may mean something that is of special significance to us, psychologically. Dreams, especially such dreams, should be noted and respected, although we should hesitate to make final judgement as to their meaning. Some dreams may also be prophetic, and these may be the noticeable, memorable dreams, or they may not. Only by noting dreams and looking for events they portend can we be sure. In this way the prophetic dreams may become more noticeable and momentous. Some people are naturally gifted with the ability to 'dream true' and awaken knowing they have just had a prophetic dream, while in others the ability may need to be coaxed out. The entire territory of dreams is a fertile one, for while sleeping we are floating in the instinctual realm. Dreams are by no means untainted by our daily life and its petty stresses and preoccupations, but they are still close to Otherworld.

Incubation was another technique favoured by Nostradamus, which is little more than 'sleeping on it'. If you want the answer to a question, meditate on it before going to sleep and saturate yourself with the thought, writing the question on a piece of paper and putting it under your pillow. It is important, if you do this, not to be tense and wound-up so that you do not sleep properly, and the question simply runs through your mind all night, for that way all you'll have when you wake up is a headache. You need to be clear about the question, relaxed and able to sleep deeply. Here we are not looking for a dream. If this works for you, you will wake up knowing the answer, or with some strong feeling about the matter, which you should write down before it gets contaminated by waking

doubts and consciousness. Like all approaches, this can be developed with practice.

SCRYING

Scrying is the process of looking for images in a reflective surface, such as Nostradamus may have done with his *mirouer ardant*. For this you may use a dark mirror, a crystal, or a bowl of water. Some people like to drop into the water something that shines, such as a silver ring. Silver, by the way, is to be preferred over gold and other metals for this purpose, as silver is linked to the Moon, which in turn is linked to the instinctual night-time areas of the brain. The object used for scrying is known as a speculum, and there are many varieties, from glass bottles to fishermen's floats.

Scrying is a very ancient practise, possibly as old as the human race, because it is a process for opening the inner sight. The Elizabethan occultist, John Dee, used a crystal globe or shew-stone and also a dark mirror, possibly made of jet. If you are serious about scrying then you should choose a speculum with care, consecrate it at Full Moon and keep it wrapped in a black cloth, never exposing it to sunlight.

Moonlight, however, will do it nothing but good and you may 'charge it up' by leaving it in the rays of the moon. Rituals for cleaning and consecration can be found by consulting *Witchcraft: A Beginner's Guide*; *Spells and Rituals: A Beginner's Guide* and *Witchcraft: A Complete Guide* by Teresa Moorey, all published by Hodder & Stoughton. You may simply psychically cleanse your speculum by leaving it in salt water for several hours, drying it with a clean piece of muslin and keeping it wrapped in black cloth until you are ready to consecrate it, which you should do at Full Moon. Light a candle, burn a joss-stick or incense and affirm that this speculum is to be used by you, wisely and with the purest motives, as a means to revelation. Always keep your speculum wrapped and out of the way, until you wish to use it, and do not let anyone else touch it.

When intending to scry, choose a dim light, the source of which is behind you. Candlelight is best. Some people like the light to fall on the speculum, others prefer the surface to remain blank. In all things you must choose what works best for you. It is a good idea to burn a joss-stick or incense. All incense has mind-altering qualities in the sense that scent activates the instinctual part of the brain, but a blend of mugwort, wormwood and sandalwood is to be recommended. Please remember that the first two smell awful! If you burn incense you are more closely imitating the Seer of Salon himself! Now you will need to remember what you have learnt about being relaxed and detached, so that you are in the correct frame of mind. Please do not stare into the speculum not daring to blink! Just look naturally and attentively. You may need lots of practice with this, and no two people will have exactly the same experience. If you do not see anything, give up after half an hour at the most and try again another day.

The speculum should eventually seem to become misty and then something will appear, possibly very indistinct or meaningless at first. Sometimes what you see will be 'inward' in that you will see an image in your mind. At other times you may literally seem to see something. Whatever the case, do not necessarily be in a hurry to interpret what you see, unless this seems plain – sometimes a feeling of inner certainty is part of the experience, at other times definitely not. Remember also that what you see may well be symbolic, so don't be too literal and/or hasty, especially at first. In addition, it may not be about 'the future' as such, but the present or even the past, and most of what is apprehended may be very personal. You can approach your scrying for the answer to a specific question or just as a general 'look-see' which witches may do at Hallowe'en. When you have finished your scrying, put your speculum away with care, and ground yourself in the ways mentioned.

FINAL WORD

Any method of foretelling the future needs to be approached sensibly. Ask yourself if you really want to develop this gift, for it can bring problems. Whatever you do, do it responsibly and with circumspection. The gift of prophecy is a dangerous one where it is cultivated to pander to the ego and to glamorise. It is fine to feel proud of your developing talents, but keep this in proportion! And do not get so carried away that you forget the ordinary things in life, for you need a healthy and sensible lifestyle to keep you grounded.

The remaining chapters of the book look at selected prophecies from the most well-known of Nostradamus' works, the Centuries. *However, it should be borne in mind that he also wrote the* Presages, *the* Sixains *and other, shorter writings containing prophecy, including the* Letter à Henri II.

Current scientific knowledge gives little protection against floods, earthquakes and tornadoes. In addition, during our times there is much fear of massive natural disaster that has the potential for wiping out most, if not all, of the life on earth. This fear stems partly from a general millennarian anxiety and a dread of the end of the world that has been foretold in many quarters, and also because of our guilt, as a species, for the harm that we are doing, and continue to do, to the earth. Advancing knowledge also contributes to our fears as we amass data on the K/T boundary event, the collision

Henri II of France.

with an asteroid that may have killed the dinosaurs, 65 million years ago. In *The Mars Mystery* (by Graham Hancock, Robert Bauvel and John Grigsby, Penguin, 1998), a convincing theory regarding general threat from asteroids is put forward, describing how a collision with one may have stripped Mars of its atmosphere, and its life, many millions of years ago. Evidence is also growing to suggest that there may have been a pole shift in Earth's remote past. A substantial, sudden movement in the poles of the Earth's revolution would result in tidal waves many miles high, mountains swallowed by the earth

and ferociously destructive winds. Cataclysmic events are hinted at in ancient records and the theory of Atlantis and its demise may be one such. Geological evidence bears out the possibility of pole shift. For instance, the Ice Ages came abruptly, not gradually, fossils of maritime creatures have been found hundreds of feet above the sea level and hundreds of miles inland, in North America for instance. Entire mammoth herds with vegetation still in their mouths have been unearthed in Siberia. Our concept of the Earth as *terra firma* is giving away to the uneasy impression that we live on a little globe that wobbles in space. The front pages of newspapers carry news and pictures of possible approaching asteroids. What did the seer have to say about such events, some of which he could hardly have imagined?

Century I.LXIX

La grand montaigne ronde de sept estades
Apres paix, guerre, faim, inundation:
Roulera loing abysmant grands contrades,
Mesmes antiques, & grand fondation.

A huge mountain, measuring seven stadiums in circumference
After peace war, famine and flood.
It will spread a great distance, swallowing great countries
Even ancient structures and their trusty foundations.

The irresistible interpretation of this quatrain is meteor strike. The asteroid that caused the great extinction at the Cretaceous/Tertiary boundary was caused by an object from space at least ten kilometres in diameter. It destroyed 75 per cent of species and 99.9 per cent of animals then living. The asteroid hit the Yucatan peninsula at 30km per second, causing a crater 200km in diameter. Earthquakes of a magnitude 12 to 13 on the Richter scale rumbled around the world. A tsunami more than a kilometre in height inundated the land over 800km from the point of impact. A global firestorm burnt for several days, followed by a type of 'nuclear winter', caused by dust and smoke, that lasted for several months. NASA, in collaboration with other authorities, has agreed to catalogue the characteristics of all comets and asteroids that cross the Earth's orbit and measure more than one kilometre in diameter, the reason for this being that civilisation could probably not survive

collision with an object of such dimensions. ('Seven stadiums'?) However, other interpretations have included the ubiquitous Muslim invasion, of Rome in this case, and floods on Mount Olympus following earthquakes in the Middle East.

Century I.XVII

Par quarante ans l'Iris n'aparoistra
Par quarante ans tous les jours sera veu:
La terre aride en siccite croistra
Et grans deluges quand sera aperceu.

For 40 years no rainbow will appear
For 40 years it will be seen daily:
The arid earth will become drier
And then mighty floods when it is once more seen.

The periods spoken of here are apocalyptic. This could refer to a nuclear winter, arising from conflict, meteor impact or possibly simply the greenhouse effect, which could manifest similarly if it grows unchecked. Conceivably periods of peace and war may be indicated, 1830–70, 1871–1914. Peter Lemesurier (see Further reading) links this quatrain with the following:

Century I.XCI

Les dieux feront aux humains apperence
Ce quils seront auteurs de grand conflit:
Avant ciel veu serain espee & lance
Que vers main gauche sera plus grand afflit.

The gods will make it seem to humans
That they have caused a great war:
Before the sky was free of sword and lance
And now the greatest harm will be to the left side.

This quatrain may refer to war between China and the West, with the worst casualties inflicted upon the left-hand side of the map, namely the USA. Or could 'left' mean those whose politics are to the left? The hardware in the sky sounds like rockets and missiles, appearing after a peaceful interlude. From the comment about the 'gods' the war could seem to come out of nowhere, which is possible if a country with first-strike capability mistakenly concluded it was

under attack. However, this quatrain could refer to natural disaster such as a shower of large meteorites, the 'hail out of heaven' foretold in Revelation 16:21 where each stone weighed a talent, i.e. 34kg/75lbs. Such meteor showers have been recorded during reversals, such as pole shift.

Century IX.LXXXIII

Sol vingt de taurus si fort terre trembler
Le grand theatre rempli ruinera,
L'air ciel et terre obscurcir & troubler
Lors l'infidelle Dieu et sainctz voguera.

When the sun in in 20° of Taurus there will be so strong a
*   shaking of the earth*
That the great theatre will be ruined, while full.
The air, the heavens and the earth are dark and troubled
While the Unbeliever calls on God and the saints.

An apocalyptic quatrain, which could be taken to refer to Muslim holy war, or to a massive earthquake taking place when the sun is in 20° of Taurus, which happens every year on or around May 10. There has been speculation regarding dire events in May 2000, when many planets line up in the sign of Taurus. At the beginning of the month the Sun, Moon, Mercury, Venus, Mars, Jupiter and Saturn are all in the sign, i.e. all the planets known in the time of the seer, and he may have known about this. On May 9/10 2000 the Sun, in 20° Taurus, is exactly conjunct Saturn, considered a malefic planet in the time of Nostradamus, and indeed in the present time. it is also conjunct Jupiter and Mercury. Venus is still in Taurus, but only in very wide conjunction, being 9° from the Sun, while Mars has moved into Gemini. On May 10 the Moon forms a square aspect from Leo, which may be considered stressful, and Uranus also forms a square, from Aquarius. Because the degrees involved are 18–20 of fixed signs, astrologers may feel that the stresses created by the total eclipse of the Sun, and attending aspects in August 1999, might be triggered. The August 1999 eclipse took place in 18° of Leo, the sign of Fixed Fire. Taurus is the sign of Fixed Earth. One might certainly speculate regarding possible earthquakes, especially in countries where the eclipse was visible. It is worthwhile noting that the horoscope of Turkey, cast for the proclamation of the

republic 29/10/23 in Ankara shows Neptune at 20° of Leo, and Neptune is the god of earthquakes. The chart for the UK shows Neptune in 18° of Scorpio, the sign of Fixed Water.

It is interesting that there is a massive and widespread stream of meteors, called the Taurid stream, so-called because it appears to originate in the constellation of Taurus. This intersects the orbits of Earth in two places, so we pass through it twice a year, in late June/early July and early November. However, it must be remembered that the constellation of Taurus does not correspond with the astrological sign Taurus, due to precession. There are also hints in Egyptian mythology and the alignment of the Sphinx to suggest that important astronomical events (such as meteor impact) may be connected with Taurus, the Bull of the Sky, constellation of Set the Destroyer. These matters are fully discussed in *The Mars Mystery* (see earlier). Astrologers will not feel easy about the Taurus conjunction, but such things can manifest in many different ways and different levels. By the time you read this, the matter will be history!

Century I.LXXXVII

Ennosigee feu du centre de terre
Fera trembler au tour de cite neufve:
Deux grands rochiers long temps feront la guerre
Puis Arethusa rougira nouveau fleuve.

Fire from the centre of the earth, erupting
Will cause shaking around the New City.
Two great solid powers will make war for a long time
And then Arethusa will again redden the river.

The 'new city' when written of by Nostradamus may be taken to mean New York. This may well refer to a volcanic explosion and the reddened river could be lava. This may refer to the eruption at Mount St Helens in 1980. The volcanic ash could be seen as far away as New York. There seems also to be a reference to the Cold War. Of course, World War III and a nuclear holocaust cannot be ruled out.

Arethusa, in Greek mythology, was a water nymph gifted with prophecy. This is a disturbing quatrain which may or may not already have been fulfilled.

Century X.LXVII

Le tremblement si fort au Mois de Mai
Saturne Caper, Jupiter, Mercure au beuf:
Venus aussi Cancer, Mars, en Nonnay,
Tombera gresle lors plus grosse qu'un euf

So great a shaking in the month of May
Saturn in Capricorn, Jupiter and Mercury in Taurus
Venus also in Cancer, Mars in Virgo
Hailstones larger than eggs will fall.

Yet another grim prophecy for the merry month of May! Perhaps this is a good time to remind ourselves that with Nostradamus anything may be in code, and 'May' has been interpreted as a code for '5' meaning in some places five years, or centuries. In May 2047 Saturn will be in Capricorn, Jupiter and Mercury in Taurus. However, as Venus moves into Cancer, Mercury moves out of Taurus and into Gemini. Mars is in Gemini, which has some links with Virgo in that they are both mutable signs and both ruled by Mercury. No similar configuration occurred throughout the twentieth century. Again the hail of Revelations 16.21 is indicated: 'And there fell upon men a great hail out of heaven, every stone about the weight of a talent... the plague thereof was exceeding great.' However, as we have seen a 'talent' weighs 75lbs, much bigger than an egg!

Century III.XII

Par la tumeur de Heb, Po, Tag, Timbre & Rosne
Et par l'estang Leman & Aretin
Les deux grans chefs & cites de Garonne
Prins, morts, noies. Partir humain butin.

Because of the swelling of the Egro, Po, Tagus, Tiber and the Rhône
By Lake Geneva and Arezzo
The two great leaders and the cities of the Garonne taken
Dead, drowned. Salvaged humans are shared out.

This quatrain seems to threaten substantial rise in sea levels due to global warming, which will cause the polar ice caps to melt. Scientists suggest that sea levels could rise by five metres by the end of this century. A combination of the greenhouse effect and depletion of the ozone layer could result in the flooding of great

portions of Europe. The leaders might well be taken and killed, under such circumstances. An alternative explanation offered is Muslim invasion of Europe. The last three words might be translated 'the human booty will be divided/shared out' or 'people divide the booty'. If it does mean 'human booty' could this refer to extra-terrestrials, who have been reported as using humans for experiment, 'sharing out' the remaining specimens? In *The Sirius Mystery* (Arrow, 1998), Robert Temple explores the possibility of former extra-terrestrials who were amphibious, creating a pool in which to swim, as they came out of their spacecraft. This account is preserved in the stories of the Dogon tribe, who possess astronomical knowledge that science is only now confirming, specifically about the planet Sirius from which these beings came.

Amphibious ETs in a future Waterworld – could this have been the vision of Nostradamus? It is more likely that we remain in the familiar territory of man's inhumanity to man. There is little doubt that in the face of global catastrophe we would revert to savagery, and slavery is a possibility. Alternatively, those who are rescued might be granted asylum in a variety of places worldwide.

Century V.XCVIII

A quarante huict degre climaterique
A fin de Cancer si grande seicheresse:
Poisson en mer fleuve, lac cuit hectique,
Bearn, Bigorre par feu ciel en detresse.

On the forty-eighth climacteric degree
At the end of the sign of Cancer, so great a drought.
Fish in the sea, river and lake violently boiled.
Distress to Bearn and Bigorre from fire in the sky.

This suggests global warming and its effects. The sun reaches the end of the sign of Cancer on or around July 22 by our modern calendar – a month past midsummer and approaching the time of year when overheating would be felt at its worst in the northern hemisphere. The 48th degree of latitude runs through Rennes, Orleans and Langres. Bern, in Switzerland, is approximately 1° south. During this century, if the present rate of warming continues unabated, temperatures worldwide will increase by as much as 3°

Centigrade. This hardly constitutes 'boiling'. However, ecologically it is a very dangerous, and substantial rise which will have far-reaching effects. Conceivably, the quatrain could refer to the effects of radiation and nuclear attack.

Century II.III

Pour la chaleur solaire sus la mer
De Negrepont les poissons demis cuits:
Les habitans les viendront entamer
Quand Rod & Gennes leur faudra le biscuit.

Through the heat of the sun on the sea
The fish in Hegrepont are semi-cooked.
The inhabitants will come to eat them
When Rhodes and Genoa have no food.

Another global warming quatrain? Due to the use of fossil fuels and other factors greenhouse gases such as carbon dioxide are building up in the atmosphere causing the oceans to heat up. Marine life is already suffering, fish and coral reefs are dying as a result of the upsetting of the delicate balance necessary for survival. It seems Nostradamus foresaw the effects of pollution etc. on the environment. However, atomic explosion could be indicated, possibly in the Aegean. Other interpretations have offered impact by an asteriod and Muslim invasion of Europe as possibilities.

Century II.XLV

Trop le ciel pleure l'Androgyn procree
Pres de ce ciel sang humain respandu
Par mort trop tarde grand peuple recree
Tard & tost vient le secours attendu.

Too much weeps the sky when the Androgyne is created;
Close to the heavens human blood is spilt.
The death comes too late to revive the great nation.
Sooner or later the awaited aid arrives.

This may refer to a victorious leader – possibly a woman who looks like a man, or vice versa – who wages battle in the skies. It may also refer in some way to the modern ability to change the gender of those who wish it, and the moral dilemmas that may result. There is

no doubt that our ability to manipulate life at the genetic level is
increasing rapidly – faster, in fact, than our ability to integrate this
into our current belief structures. Many people fear that this will, in
time, result in chaos, strife and horror. Human cloning could be
involved here, possibly a warlike 'superbreed' such as 'Robocop',
'Bionic Man' or 'Universal Soldier'. There can be little doubt that
scientifically advanced countries are experimenting along these
lines. Human fertility is gradually failing, at the present time, due
probably to synthetic female hormones in the eco-system which are
being absorbed by men, and to other factors, such as pollution,
synthetic diet, etc. The 'awaited help' may well come through
science. This quatrain may conceivably refer to future contact with
ETs. It has also been linked with events following the death of the
Ayatollah Khomeini in the 1980s.

Century II.XLVI

Apres grand trouble humain, plus grands' apreste
Le grand mouteur les siecles renouvele
Pluie, sang, laict, famine, fer & peste
Au ciel veu, feu courant longue estincele.

After dire misery for humankind a greater affliction comes
As the great cycle renews the centuries.
Rain, blood, milk, famine, iron and plague
Fire seen in the sky, trailing a tail of sparks.

Comets, or 'hairy stars' were seen as harbingers of doom. This has
been taken as an Armageddon quatrain. Erika Cheetham (see
Further reading) suggests a great war occurring between the 1986
appearance of Halley's Comet and the end of the century.
Thankfully, this did not materialise. The next scheduled appearance
of the comet will be in 2062. The earlier appearance was in 1910,
before the Great War. Any modern war will involve 'fire in the sky'.

Century II.XCV

Les lieux peuple seront inhabitables:
Pour champs avoir grand division:
Regnes livres a prudents incapables:
Lors les grands freres mort & dissension.

> *Populated areas will become uninhabitable*
> *Great dissent to obtain land.*
> *Sovereignty given to those incapable of prudence*
> *Then death and dissension for the powerful brothers.*

Destruction of the environment is again heralded, with good land in short supply. In the time of Nostradamus the population of the world stood at under 500 million. No destruction of the environment worth speaking of had taken place. Five hundred years later, by 2050, the population is projected to have increased to 10 billion, meanwhile land may have been destroyed by intensive farming. The great brothers may be the Kennedys, although how this might tie in with the rest of the quatrain is unclear. This quatrain has also been linked to a third world war in Palestine, the collapse of the US/Soviet alliance and the aftermath of Muslim invasion of France.

Century I.LXVII

La grand famine que je sens approcher
Souvent tourner, puis estre universele:
Si grande & longue qu'on viendra arracher
Du bois racine, & l'enfant de mammelle.

The great famine that I sense is on its way
Often intermittent will then become universal:
So vast and long lasting that they will tear
Roots from the wood and the baby from the breast.

Again Nostradamus foretells of great shortage of food in some future time. Because of the rapid growth in population, and because of modern farming methods and the exploitation of the Third World by developed countries, famine is indeed widespread, especially in Africa. Famine occurs in parts of China, sporadically, as the population is concentrated on the floodplains of rivers where conditions are unstable. The fear here is that the only way for the people to survive will be to expend into other countries. Although famine was common in the sixteenth century, it does seem that Nostradamus was giving warning of something worse. Indeed, it is happening before our very eyes.

There is a moral imperative for developed countries to take action. Was the prophet giving us fair warning?

4

NOSTRADAMUS AND WAR

*T*he latter half of the twentieth century was overshadowed by the
threat of a third world war and a nuclear holocaust. Many people
have examined the words of Nostradamus with trepidation, to decipher
the prophecies of the seer. As we pass into the twenty-first century the
gloomy, paranoid days of the Cold War seem far in the past. However,
conflicts continue worldwide and while weapons of mass destruction
exist there is always the possibility that they will be unleashed. Let us
first look at a couple of quatrains about former wars that appear to
have been fulfilled.

Century V.LXXXI

L'oiseau royal sur la cite solaire
Sept moys devant fera nocturne augure:
Mur d'Orient cherra tonnairre, esclaire,
Sept jours aux portes les ennem a l'heure.

Over the city of the sun will fly the royal bird
Seven months beforehand it will make nightly prophecy:
The Eastern wall with fall, thunder and lightning
In seven days the enemies stand at the gates.

This quatrain seems to fit certain events early on in World War II very well. The 'royal bird' is the German Eagle, and from December 1939 to April 1940 German planes flew regularly over Paris, dropping propaganda leaflets and even prophecies by Nostradamus, interpreted as foretelling French defeat. The 'Eastern walls' refers to the Maginot Line, which was breached during the Blitzkrieg, seven days lasting from June 5–11, 1940, leaving Paris open to invasion. Earlier interpretations suggested the fall of the Berlin Wall, but now that has long taken place the verse does not seem to fit. However, the quatrain has also been suggested to presage Muslim invasion of France at Lyon.

Century II.XXIIII

Bestes farouches de faim fluves tranner:
Plus part du camp encontre Hister sera,
En caige de fer le grand fera treisner
Quand Rin enfant Germain observera.

Beasts, mad with hunger will cross the rivers
Most of the battlefield will be against Hister
In a cage of iron the great one will be dragged
When the German child sees nothing.

This quatrain is one of the most famous. The Latin name for the Danube, which flows near Hitler's childhood home in Linz in Austria, is Ister. The wife of Goebbels, Hitler's propaganda minister, brought these lines to the attention of her husband, who made capital out of them. However, as it transpired, it was the body of the German ally, Mussolini, whose body appeared in an 'iron cage' – the charred remains of a bombed petrol station. The German people indeed did 'see nothing', being led like children by their leader. The first line refers to the Russian soldiers who raped some 50,000 German women after they crossed the Elbe in revenge for the ghastly Siege of Stalingrad. Out of the population of 500,000 only

1,515 people remained alive, and some of the survivors had turned to cannibalism. War had made beasts of all those involved.

However, as we have seen in Chapter 2, it is unlikely that Nostradamus meant anything but a river when he spoke of 'Hister', and there are other interpretations of this quatrain. Peter Lemesurier (see Further reading) interprets this as a possible Muslim invasion of Hungary in 2000, and it may refer to any one of several episodes in World War II.

Century X.LXXII

L'an mil neuf cens nonante neuf sept mois
Du ciel viendra un grand Roy deffraieur
Resusciter le grand Roy d'Angolmois
Avant apres Mars regner par bon heur.

In the seventh month of the year 1999
From the sky will come a great deffraying king
To revive the king of Angolmois
Before and after Mars rules happily.

As the last year of the millennium unfolded this quatrain was widely discussed, causing not a little disquiet. Because of alterations in the calendar since the time of Nostradamus the solar eclipse on August 11 would, by earlier calculations, have occurred in July, the 'seventh month'. The eclipse was accompanied by what astrologers call a Grand Cross, meaning four or more planets at right angles to one another in the sky, and one of these was Mars, in its 'night house', Scorpio. It is possible that Nostradamus would have known, from contemporary tables, that Mars would have been in Scorpio, although it is unlikely he would have been aware of the degree. Saturn in Taurus opposed Mars, and both planets squared the eclipse point, Sun and Moon in Leo. Because of the eclipse cycle discovered by the Greek, Meton, Nostradamus would possibly have known about the eclipse itself, and while Uranus, the other planet involved in the Grand Cross, had not yet been discovered, the configuration would still have looked somewhat 'nasty' coming as it did at the end of the millennium. 'Angolmois' has been taken as an anagram of 'Mongolois' – such imperfect anagrams were used by the seer at times.

This quatrain is useful as an illustration of the ease with which Nostradamus can be misinterpreted. Some editions print 'deffraieur' as *d'effraieur* changing possible translations from 'deffraying', i.e. 'peacemaking', to 'fearful', 'a great king of fear'. This mistake is still appearing in books and even without the apostrophe, 'king of terror' appears as the translation. I have made the same mistake myself in *The Millennium and Beyond* (Hodder & Stoughton, 1999). With hindsight, we might link this quatrain to the war in Serbia where Allied intervention did seem to help, so 'Mars reigned happily'. No dramatic event coincided with the eclipse itself, although only the most simplistic of astrologers would have expected this, and the effects of the eclipse are still playing out, both in individual lives and collective matters. An eclipse is part of a cycle. This is confirmed by more complex astrological techniques which we do not have the space to cover. But some of the effects are good!

Century I.LXIIII

De nuit soleil penseront veu
Quand le pourceau demy-homme on verra
Bruict, chant, bataille au ciel battre aperceu
Et bestes brutes a parler lon orra.

They will think they have seen the sun at night
When they see the pig half man.
Noise, singing, battle fought in the sky
And brute beats will be heard to speak.

This quatrain has both an apocalyptic ring and a kind of nursery-rhyme quality. However, it is most interesting, for plans have already been made to construct huge mirrors that can light up the night sky in the northern hemisphere, where the sun disappears for the winter months. The half-man half-pig creature could be a reference to the development of animal organs to be used in transplant operations and one of the projects is for the use of a pig's heart. Pigs' livers have already been used. It may also refer to genetic experiments, the truth of which may be concealed from the public.

If we speculate wildly, talking animals could conceivably be created by genetic manipulation, and this could refer to bestial humans,

cloned as fighting machines. Erika Cheetham (see Further reading) makes the point that pilots in goggles and oxygen masks look like pigs, and that the noises are reminiscent of an aerial battle, with instructions coming over the radio. It is also something of a picture of modern life, as seen from the sixteenth century: the singing and noises could be broadcasts of popular music and neon lights turn night to day. However, developments that would have seemed impossible only decades ago, for example genetic engineering, making one wonder if one can sometimes take Nostradamus at his most fantastical quite literally.

Century X.LXXIIII

Au resolu du grand nombre septiesme
Apparoistra au temps Jeux d'Hacatombe,
Non esloigne du grand eage millesme,
Que les entre sortiront de leur tombe.

At the completion of the great seventh in number
It will appear at the time of the Hacatombe games
Not far from the time of the millennium
That those within the tomb come out.

This may be a vision of the year 7000, when science is able to raise the dead from their graves. It is an apocalyptic quatrain, and may foretell the end of the world, when the dead will arise for the Last Judgement. 'Jeux d'Hacatombe' can be translated as 'games of slaughter' or 'sacrificial games'. 'Hekatombe' is a Greek word meaning 100 oxen, such as were sacrificed to the goddess in Crete, and so may mean ritual slaughter. War being a 'game' this could be seen as yet another reference to bloody conflict. Erika Cheetham interprets this quatrain as large-scale war breaking out at the end of the 1970s, with the final war occurring at the millennium. While it is true that conflict is ever present, this has not yet materialised. However, as we have seen, Nostradamus is not obvious and the reference to the number seven could mean many things. The 'seventh millennium' after the biblical creation of the world, calculated according to the Book of Enoch was explained by Nostradamus in his letter to Henri II, will occur on or around 2828 CE.

Century II.XXII

Le camp Asop d'Eurotte partira
S'adjoignant proche de l'isle submergee:
D'Arton classe phalange pliera
Nombril du monde plus grand voix subrogee.

The pointless army will depart out of Europe
Reforming near the submerged island
The ranks of the NATO fleet will fold
Overcome by a greater voice in the navel of the world.

The interpretation of this rests on 'D'Arton' being an anagram of NATO/OTAN. It may also and alternatively refer to a bread-giving, hence life-giving, fleet. The submerged island is taken to be Britain, but some interpretations have suggested Atlantis, so presumably placing events in the Atlantic. (Note: serious modern reasearchers who believe there may indeed be a 'lost continent' do not necessarily place this in the Atlantic.) This quatrain could mean the end of NATO. Russia is pressurising for a new alliance that better represents the state of affairs now that the Cold War and the USSR are things of the past. The fleet may be on an exercise, hence 'pointless'. The 'navel of the world' could mean Italy. Erika Cheetham also suggests the Middle East as the cradle of civilisation. Some greater power overcomes the fleet, therefore. This could mean that the USA takes over the Persian Gulf, an invasion of the Middle East or an invasion by the Warsaw Pact countries that leads to World War III. It could also refer to many accidents that have surrounded events in the Middle East over the last few years, or in years to come. The 'greater voice' from Italy could mean that of the pope in Rome. Many interpretations are possible.

Century II.XCVI

Flambeau ardent au ciel soir sera veu
Pres de la fin & principe du Rosne:
Famine, glaive: tard le secours pourveu
La Perse tourne envahir Macedoine.

A flame will be seen burning in the evening sky
The length of the Rhône
Famine and weaponry: help is provided late
Persia turns to invade Macedonia.

The last line of this quatrain appears very clear in that Persia, i.e. modern-day Iran, reverses history. The conquering Macedonian, Alexander the Great, burnt Persepolis in 330 BCE, while drunk. Now the tables will be turned by some form of counter-invasion. Macedonia is unstable, being part of the former Yugoslavia, and it is not unlikely that it will be taken over by Islam, or a Muslim country. War and strife elsewhere may mean that help arrives very late. The quatrain appears to be referring to the ongoing conflict in the Balkans, and may refer to aerial battles and severe bombing *flambeau ardent au ciel* – seen as lights in the sky. It may also refer to terrorist attack, or Muslim invasion of Europe.

Century VI.XXIIII

Mars & le sceptre se trouvera conjoinct,
Dessoubz Cancer calamitouse guerre
Un peu apres sera nouveau Roy oingt
Qui par long temps pacifiera la terre.

Mars and Jupiter will be in conjunction
And under Cancer there will be a calamitous war.
A little afterwards a new king will be anointed
Who will bring peace on earth for a long period.

Mars and Jupiter come into conjunction at intervals of just over two years, and the Sun is in Cancer between the dates of June 22 to July 23, approximately, each year. If this quatrain refers to a Jupiter–Mars conjunction in Cancer this will happen in early July, 2002. This seems to be a fairly straightforward quatrain, encouragingly, promising a reign of peace after war. This may also refer to someone who will redeem the world by his/her leadership. We are not really told where the war will be, but, Muslim invasion of Europe has been suggested as a possibility. In the time of Nostradamus, the Muslims were, in fact, continually engaged in invasion. At present we may still consider fundamentalist factions a great threat, if not through all-out overt war then via a campaign of terrorism. Danger will always persist where any strong and determined group of people regard the material world – arguably the supreme gift of deity – as something essentially vile, to be denied and subdued. Such an approach denies the body, and frequently extremist followers are quite willing to wreak any form of destruction on themselves and

others in hope of the blessings of an Afterlife. Nostradamus, with his Jewish ancestry, must have been very well aware of the suffering that derives from dogmatism and prejudice of all kinds.

However, while *le sceptre* is an acceptable code for Jupiter, being the planet named after the ruler of the Olympian gods, one can only wonder at the apparent obvious nature of this quatrain which is not typical of Nostradamus' style.

Century II.XXX

Un qui les dieux d'Annibal infernaulx
Fera renaistre, effrayeur des humains,
Onq' plus d'horreurs ne plus pire journaux
Qu'avint viendra par Babel aux Romains.

One through whom the infernal gods of Hannibal
Will be reborn, the terror of humankind.
Even greater horror, papers have never described
Worse than will come, through Babel, to the Romans.

Hannibal (247–183 BCE) was the general from Carthage who came perilously close to conquering Rome by marching across the Alps in 218 BCE. The consternation caused to the Romans by this fearless invader with his elephants may be imagined. This predicted invader will invoke similar fears, attempting, possibly successfully, the seemingly impossible. 'Babel' indicates that people of diverse tongues will be united and involved in this invasion, which has been interpreted as coming to Europe from an Eastern superpower. As Hannibal came from North Africa, we might also expect trouble from that quarter. As newspapers did not exist in the time of Nostradamus his use of *journaux* is interesting and possibly futuristic, the only sixteenth-century parallel being pamphlets. This quatrain could mean the general collapse of religions, especially the Catholic Church, 'Romains'. Other interpretations include, of course, Muslim invasion of Europe, the specific destruction of Catholicism by a leader from North Africa, war on Italy by oil-rich countries, and the coming of the antichrist.

Century VI.XXI

Quant ceulx de polle arctiq unus ensemble
En Orient grand effraieur & crainte
Esleu nouveau sustenu le grand temple
Rode, Bisance de sang Barbare taincte.

When those of the Arctic pole come together
In the East will be great terror and fear.
The newly elect will find support in the establishment.
Rhodes and Byzantium stained with the blood of the Barbarian.

This may be linked to quatrain VI.V, which is discussed in Chapter 5. It may simply echo the meaning of countries being united in the face of some sort of modern plague, such as AIDS. However, it may also relate to the ending of the Cold War, the initiatives made by Bush and Gorbachev and possible unease in China. If and when the time comes that Russia and Western powers are truly united, Nostradamus may have foreseen that China will be truly filled with dread, and thus possibly more warlike. The resulting polarisation of forces may mean that the eyes of the superpowers move away from the Middle East, war breaks out anew between Turkey and Greece and the Arabs invade. To Nostradamus, the Arabs would have seemed like barbarians, because of their non-Christian beliefs. Nostradamus was of Jewish ancestry and may well have harboured sympathies with the Muslims, who, during their occupation of southern Europe were far more tolerant than the Christians. It has also been suggested that he may have played an important part in a secret society with beliefs that are/were certainly 'heretical' by mainstream Christian standards. For further details you may consult *The Holy Blood and the Holy Grail* (Arrow, 1996). This quatrain could mean the start of World War III, the newly elected one presumably being a military or political leader, sanctioned possibly by the Church.

5

NOSTRADAMUS
AND DISEASE

*A*s we have seen, disease in the days of Nostradamus was
*potentially a ghastly matter for entire communities, on the scale of
war or natural disaster. Thus, the prophet lived with a perspective on
disease that is largely irrelevant in modern times, in the developed
world. However, we still live with the possibility of large-scale
pestilence, of one sort or another, and genetically modified bugs,
superbugs, radiation sickness, chemical poisoning or similar could
afflict us in the twenty-first century. These are often the subject of
morbid fears, science fiction or simple speculation, based sometimes on
the words of the prophet himself. Let us look at a few quatrains that
may relate to disease.*

Century II.IX

Neuf ans le regne le maigre en paix tiendra
Puis il cherra en soif si sanguinaire
Pour luy grand peuple sans foy & loy mourra
Tue par un beaucoup plus de bonnaire.

The reign of the thin one holds sway for nine years
Then it will fall into a thirst so bloody
That for it a great nation without faith or law will pass away
Slain by one who is much more alluring.

Erica Cheetham (see Further reading) links this quatrain with AIDS. In Africa, where it started, AIDS was known as the 'thin disease' or the 'slim disease', *maigre* meaning 'thin'. It is unclear whether the term 'nine years' relates to the life expectancy of the person diagonised with the disease or the length of time before the disease is/was discovered. Research in the 1980s indicated that 99 per cent of those infected are likely to die within a decade. The 'great nation', 'grand peuple' could refer to Africa or the USA, conceivably, or to a decimation of the homosexual community. However, while AIDS is a very real threat since its emergence in the 1980s, deaths have not reached the huge numbers feared by some and new discoveries have been made about the disease, for instance, that some people may carry a natural immunity. As for the final line 'slain by one who is more alluring/charming/gracious', this could refer to the person who eventually finds a cure.

However, the entire quatrain may refer to something else altogether, for instance the reign of Louis XVI.

Century II.LXXVIII

Le grand Neptune, du profond de la mer
De gent Punique & sang Gauloys mesle
Les Isles a sang, pour le tardif ramer:
Plus luy nuira que l'occult mal cele.

Great Neptune, from the sea's depths
Mixed African and French blood
The Islands remain bloodly because of the tardy one;
This will harm him more than the poorly concealed secret.

Again Erika Cheetham makes a possible link to AIDS, the secret of its victims that is badly concealed, and could be called 'the slow one'. However, it has been suggested that this could equally well refer to the much-feared Muslim invasion of Europe. It could also refer to the Barbary pirates, based in North Africa.

Century III.LXXV

Pau, Verone, Vicence, Sarragouse,
De glaifves loings terroirs de sang humides:
Peste si grande viendra a la grand gousse
Proche secours & bien loing les remedes.

Pau, Verona, Vicenza, Saragossa
Bloody terror from distant lands
A great plague shall come in the great shell
Help is near but cure is far away.

The 'great shell' may refer to some aircraft carrying chemical warfare. The cities mentioned are European, and this could refer to war waged from a distant country, namely China. However, AIDS is also indicated, *peste si grande*, for which some help is near, in that the HIV-positive condition can be stabilised by drugs but not cured, and a complete cure for AIDS is a long time coming.

Century IX.LV

L'horrible guerre qu'en l'occident s'apreste
L'an ensuivant viendra la pestilence
Si fort horrible que jeune, vieulx, ne beste
Sang, feu, Mercure, Mars, Jupiter en France.

The ghastly war which arises in the west
The following year plague will come
So very horrible that not young, old or beast
Blood, fire, Mercury, Mars, Jupiter in France.

(As France was considered linked to the sign Aries, we may read here *Mercury, Mars and Jupiter in Aries*. We may also acceptably insert 'can survive' after *beste*.)

This may relate to a future war, followed by plague, conceivably related to atomic fall-out or chemical weapons. It is one of the quatrains that has been suggested may relate to Muslim invasion of

Europe and the planetary positions given suggest this may take place in the year 2011 or 2012, when this line-up next occurs. It also fits with World War I and the following epidemic of Spanish Flu. However, it may also refer to the AIDS virus. Erika Cheetham observes that one theory regarding the origin of AIDS is that it mutated from the Green Monkey, indigenous to Africa. This is actually rather a dire quatrain that possibly has not yet been fulfilled.

Century VI.V

Si grand famine par unde pestifere
Par pluye longue le long du polle arctique
Samarobryn cent lieux de l'hemispere
Vivront sans loy exemp de pollitique.

By a pestilential wave, so great a famine
Comes through a long rain, up to the North Pole.
Samarobryn, a hundred leagues above the hemisphere
They will live without laws and free from politics.

Here we have a forecast of a great disease that will apparently strike the entire northern hemisphere. Could this be as a result of extra-terrestrial attack, by an orbiting spacecraft? Or perhaps a type of biological star wars? One might speculate about the after-effects of the earth being struck by a giant meteorite, 'long rains' falling, contaminated by dust, chemicals and bacteria, where the only people to survive are those in an orbiting space station called 'Samarobryn'. Conceivably, this could also warn to the effects of severe pollution, acid rain or a Chernobyl-type disaster, where the whole hemisphere becomes contaminated. The quatrain may alternatively refer to the Russian Revolution. However, Erika Cheetham links this to AIDS and to research on AIDS carried out in an orbiting space station. She makes the point that 'Samarobryn' could be an amalgam of 'suramin' and 'ribavirin', two drugs used against AIDS. This quatrain does seem to be foretelling some future great plague, such as we might indeed expect from the interference with nature by the developed world. There must always be a possibility that some antibiotic-resistant strain may mutate as a result of this, or possibly arise in the depleted rain forests, spreading

north due to weather conditions. But this is pure speculation. From the original French it is not totally certain that anything is 'in orbit', and an event already past may be indicated.

Century V.XC

Dans les cyclades, en perinthe & larisse
Dedans Sparte tout le Pelloponnesse:
Si grande famine, peste, par faulx connisse,
Neuf moys tiendra & tout le cherrouesse.

So great a famine, plague brought by false dust
In the Cyclades, Perinthus, Larissa
In Sparta and throughout the Pelloponnessus
This will last nine months and affect the whole peninsula.

'False dust' certainly sounds like a pollutant of some kind. Conceivably it could also mean fall-out. Chemical warfare is another reasonable speculation. Whatever the disaster may be, it affects Greece and the southern Balkans, and echoes other predictions of trouble in the Middle East.

Century VII.XXI

Au port de Agde trois fustes enteront
Portant l'enfect non foy et pestilence
Passant le port mil milles embleront
Et le pont rompre a tierce resistance.

Into the port of Agde will come three shallow vessels
Bringing malice, infection and plague.
Passing the bridge they will slay a million.
The bridge will be broken by the third attempt.

Erika Cheetham makes the point that the sheer number of deaths sounds like a disaster of the twentieth century (or, for that matter, the twenty-first). This could again be some form of biological warfare, introduced cunningly by means of ocean-going vessels, carrying off large numbers of the populace. However, huge numbers of people did die from the plague in the time of the seer. This has been interpreted as relating to a third world war, and/or a Muslim invasion of France. Agde might not necessarily mean that actual place, but a similar one, such as Aden, Agadir etc. However, Ned

Halley (see Further reading) feels that this quatrain refers to a nuclear disaster, scheduled for the early years of the twenty-first century, the 'three shallow vessels' being the three cooling towers of the reactor. In this disaster, involving possibly the great reactor on the mouth of the Gironde, 20 miles from Bordeaux, pollution would be spread through waterways, including the Canal du Midi which enters the ocean ten miles south of Agde. This interpretation may link with quatrains I.XC and VI.XCVIII, which we do not have the space to cover. Other commentators do not agree, linking these two quatrains with past events. Because of the ever-present possibility of nuclear disaster it is always tempting to read this into Nostradamus.

Century IX.XI

Le juste a tort a mort lon viendra mettre
Publiquement & due mullieu estaint:
Si grande peste en ce lieu viendra naistre,
Que les jugeans fouyr seront constraint.

They will come to put the innocent one to death
Wrongfully and publicly
Such a great pestilence will come into being here
That those who judged will be put to flight.

A quatrain here that is generally believed to relate to a past event, namely the execution of King Charles I, who was publicly beheaded. Following this the Great Plague of London ravaged the city in 1655–6.

Century IX.LXXXII

Par le deluge et pestilence forte
La cite grande de long temps assiegee
La sentinelle & garde de main morte,
Subite prinse, mais de nul oultragee.

A great city lies besieged
By flood and dire pestilence for a long time.
The guards are slain by hand
And there is sudden capture, but no atrocity.

This quatrain may be a failed one. It does not seem to have been fulfilled, as, sadly, cities do not tend to be captured without atrocity. This may refer to a city that is destroyed by the breaking of a dam –

possibly Los Angeles, in which case we might speculate that the city had been under siege by the threat of earthquakes, which now destroy the dam. Disease might certainly pose a threat, as many of the hospitals and services lie on the San Andreas fault line and could be the first things to disappear. Because of the reference to pestilence it is tempting also to link this with a Third World disaster, where flooding usually spreads disease. However, Paris is often thought of as being the 'great city' for Nostradamus, and while it has certainly suffered flood, plague and invasion on numerous occasions, these have involved outrages.

Century IX XCI

L'horrible peste, Perynte et Nicopolle
Le Chersonnez tiendra et Marceloyne
La Thessalie vastera l'Amphipolle
Mal incogneu & le refus d'Anthoine.

The ghastly plague, Perinthus and Nicopolis
It was seize the peninsula and Macedonia
And will devastate Thessaly and Amphibolis
Evil unknown and Anthony's refusal.

An epidemic or disease involving Greece and part of former Macedonia is indicated. Erika Cheetham suggests that 'Anthoine' may be Antoine de Navarre, father of Henri IV, but it is unclear what the quatrain may signify in this case. A Muslim invasion of Greece after the year 2000 is reasonably suggested by Peter Lemesurier. However, perhaps the most interesting suggestion is made by Ned Halley, who interprets 'Anthoine' as Tony Blair, British Prime Minister and an important influence in NATO. Serbian intentions in the Balkans may be part of the picture, and as we well know global conflict may be provoked by such issues. The 'refusal' by 'Anthony' may be pivotal in the matter of world peace.

Century X.LXV

O vaste Romme ta ruyne s'approche
Non de tes murs de ton sang et sustence:
L'aspre par lettres fera si horrible coche,
Fer poinctu mis a tous jusques au manche.

O great Rome, your ruin is coming.
Not of your buildings, of your blood and substance.
The cruel one, by letters will make so horrible a cut
Sharp steel against all, as far as the sleeve.

This may relate to the attempted assassination of Pope John Paul II. There was a publicised attempt in Rome by a member of the Bulgarian Secret Service and a less well-known attack by one of the priests in his entourage who attempted to stab him with a weapon concealed up his sleeve – the favourite hiding-place for the assassin's knife. However, the 'up the sleeve' image has all-too-familiar modern connotations of the drug addict's syringe, which spreads AIDS and other diseases. Drugs themselves may be regarded as a plague. Ned Halley observes that AIDS does not attack from outside on the 'buildings' or 'walls' of the human body, but from within, on the very blood and substance of the human being. 'Rome' may be a metaphor of some kind, possibly of the establishment, of all that is sacred, or it may mean the undermining of Church itself by AIDS.

However, the quatrain may alternatively refer to an edict that damages the Church. In Pope John XXIII's Second Vatican Council in 1962, modernisation of the Church was attempted and this caused a schism, 'so horrible a cut'. The council was dubbed heretical by 'the Priestly Fraternity' of St Pius X led by Archbishop Marcel Lefebvre, who was subsequently suspended from his duties in 1972. Alternatively this may refer to a future event, foreshadowing the demise of the Catholic Church.

6 NOSTRADAMUS IN PERSPECTIVE

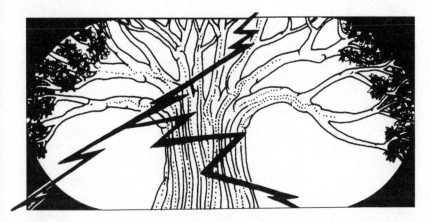

*T*he previous chapters have given a taster from the predictions of
Nostradamus. It is all too easy to read our own hopes and fears
into his words, and these vary according to contemporary
preoccupations. For instance, we have seen how the Germans
interpreted his verses to further their own ends. The Allies used them
similarly, the Americans even employed MGM to make the most of the
material!

Writers of a decade ago were full of fears about AIDS and nuclear
disaster, and while these have not gone away, the current
preoccupation relates more to the environment, pollution,
deforestation and depletion of the ozone layer. So often the
prophecies seem to relate to military threat from the Middle East.
While the Middle East is dangerously unstable, it must be

remembered that the Muslims have menaced Europe since their final expulsion from Granada on Jan 2, 1492. For folk like Nostradamus this was essentially unfortunate, for the Moors had been tolerant, their Christian successors were not, and all the Jews were expelled from the country. Despite his Catholic upbringing Nostradamus may have just a little ambivalence on the subject.

The prophecies seem full of blood and fire. It is all to easy to adopt a tabloid mentality. However, Nostradamus does also predict a Golden Age of peace, when conflict will be at an end and humans live in harmony.

Century X.LXXXIX

De brique en marbre seront les murs reduits
Sept & cinquante annees pacifique
Joie aux humains renoue Laqueduict
Sante, grandz fruict joye & temps melifique.

Brick walls will be rebuilt in marble
Fifty-seven years of peace
Joy to humans, the aqueduct rebuilt.
Health, much fruit, joy and sweet times.

This is self-explanatory. Let us hope that, as usual with Nostradamus, 57 means something else, something longer!

Century V.XLI

Nay soubs les umbres & journee nocturne
Sera en regne & bonte souveraine
Fera renaistre son sang de l'antique urne,
Renouvelant siecle d'or pour l'aerain.

Born under shadows when day is as night
One will be a sovereign, in rulership and goodness.
His/her blood will be reborn from the ancient urn
Renewing the golden century from the brass.

It seems all will be made new and peaceful by a great leader whose lineage is most ancient. Nostradamus may have meant the birth of a future 'king' in France, taking over from the crumbling republic in the twenty-first century for the salvation of Europe.

Woodcut portrait of Nostradamus.

Finally, it must be noted that the job of the prophet is to warn. If a prophet is genuine, his or her intention is to be proved wrong, rather than right by having the prophecies attended to. Many people are of the opinion that the prophecies of Nostradamus have decreased in accuracy since the 1970s, due to a raising of the human consciousness which has averted possible disaster. In the end, our attention to prophecy needs to be about more than fascination with the process. It needs to develop into the sort of cosmic consciousness and perception of essential human brother and sisterhood that makes war and destruction an impossibility.

Let us leave Nostradamus with the quatrain in which he may have been foretelling the breaking of the code to his prophecies.

Century I.XXVII

Dessousbz de chaine Guien du ciel frappe
Non loing de la est cache le tresor:
Qui pour longs siecles avoit este grappe
Trouve mourra l'oeil creve de ressort.

The treasure is hidden not far from the mistletoe-oak
Which has been struck by lightning:
That which had been hidden for long centuries now found
One dies, the eye pierced by a spring.

Ned Halley feels this quatrain relates to the document that investigators have sought, written by Nostradamus revealing the secrets of his code and the knowledge that underlies his predictions. No one can be sure whether this document exists. Here we have the hint of where it might be, but also that the site is protected by some sort of trap. Once found, this treasure will lay bare all the true meanings of the predictions. Mistletoe was considered sacred by the druids, as being a symbol of the entry into time and into incarnation of the spirit. Mistletoe meant fertility as much of the creative intellect as the body. 'Guien' may mean the ancient province of Guienne, but more probably means 'giu' which is mistletoe. The lightning strike is also symbolic of revelation. The 'one who dies' may die to ordinary life after having a mystical experience, and the 'eye pierced by a spring' may hint at scrying. Perhaps after all the 'key' to the prophecies is the opening of the inner eye of the reader.

FURTHER READING AND RESOURCES

FURTHER READING

The Final Prophecies of Nostradamus, Erika Cheetham, Futura, 1990.
An interesting look at the *Centuries* by this well-known author on the subject.

The Complete Prophecies of Nostradamus – Millennium Edition, Ned Halley (ed.), Wordsworth Reference, 1999.

The Secrets of Nostradamus, David Ovason, Century, 1997.
A fascinating and erudite look at the codes of Nostradamus.

The Nostradamus Encyclopedia, Peter Lemesurier, Thorsons, 1997.
An extremely thorough and authoritative work, covering the seer's life and times, approaches to the prophecies and detailing all the prophecies, including the *Presages* and *Sixains*. Recommended for serious study of Nostradamus.

The Essential Nostradamus, Peter Lemesurier, Piatkus, 1999.
A great book for formulating your own approach to the prophecies, with a common-sense approach to the prophet and his works.

The Millennium and Beyond: The Prophecies, Your Potential, Teresa Moorey, Hodder & Stoughton, 1999.
A discussion of various themes of the millennium, including Nostradamus, making a framework for personal growth.

The Dreamer of the Vine, Liz Greene, Corgi, 1980.
A vivid and unforgettable novel, portraying the seer at the heart of the mystery and intrigue of the period, and of secrets eternal.

The Sirius Mystery, Robert Temple, Arrow, 1998.

The Holy Blood and the Holy Grail, M. Baigent, R. Leigh and H. Lincoln, Arrow, 1996.

Resources

Maison de Nostradamus, rue Nostradamus, 13300 Salon-de-Provence, France. Source for information/publications on the seer. Series of magazines available, *Cahiers Nostradamus*.

Internet group: Nostradamus newsgroup at alt.prophecies.nostradamus

Websites: http://www.angelfire.com/biz/Nosty/index.html
http://www.m-m.org/
http://www.nostradamus.com

A BEGINNER'S GUIDE

WITCHCRAFT

Teresa Moorey

far from medieval supersition a fairy story, witchcraft is real, alive and growing. It is a religion of Nature-worship that exalts and feminine, encourages individuality and delights in celebration – and yes, it is also about magic, for magic itself is a natural force.

If you are attracted to the magical and mystical, if you have ever been alone in the countryside yet feel you were not alone – or if you are simply curious about natural forces, this is the book for you.

Witchcraft has much to offer if you practice it sincerely. It is remarkably ancient, but its message is deeply meaningful today as we realise how far we have become estranged from our roots.

A BEGINNER'S GUIDE

Ghosts

Teresa Moorey

Many of us have experienced phenomena we cannot explain by conventional means. Here, best-selling author Teresa Moorey takes a common-sense look at what has remained hidden for too long, unexplored and mysterious: the world of ghosts.

- Investigate different types of ghosts.
- Read about ghost hunting and ouija boards.
- Look at cultural and scientific aspects of life after death.
- Discover ways of preparing for and coping with a ghost encounter.

Simple exercises will help you increase your psychic powers and guide you in your own exploration of the world of ghosts.

Teresa Moorey is a qualified practising counsellor and astrologer and has followed the path of witchcraft and goddess worship for most of her adult life. She has written extensively on nature worship and astrology.

A BEGINNER'S GUIDE

UFOS

Teresa Moorey

Throughout history unidentified objects have been seen in the skies. Now that space travel is becoming a reality, the concept of visitors from other worlds has become more fascinating and more probable.

- Explore the history of UFOs.
- Discover the mystery of Roswell and the Philadelphia Experiment.
- Examine theories of government conspiracy surrounding aliens.

Simple exercises help you to discover more about this fascinating subject.

Teresa Moorey is a qualified practising counsellor and astrologer and her followed the path of witchcraft and goddess worship for most of her adult life. She has written extensively on nature worship and astrology.

A BEGINNER'S GUIDE

EARTH MYSTERIES

Teresa Moorey

The earth on which we live harbours many secrets. Is the earth a living being, as suggested by recent biological theories? Are there messages left for us to decode in stone circles and Neolithic mounds? What can you learn from observing the earth – can it help expand your own perspective on life itself?

This book covers a wide range of themes:
- ley lines and earth energies
- astro-archaeology, sacred landscapes and prehistoric structures
- shamanism and paganism
- dowsing, folklore, myth and tradition.

Whatever your interest in the earth and her secrets *Earth Mysteries – A Beginner's Guide* will not fail to fascinate and inspire!

A BEGINNER'S GUIDE

ASTROLOGY

Graham Boston

S ince the dawn of civilization people have seen a
reflection of life on earth in the stars. Astrology has
evolved into a rich and subtle language that gives
a new perspective on all areas of human experience.

- Look at the role of astrology in our lives.
- Discover how to understand and interpret a horoscope.
- Learn how to cast a horoscope.

Simple and practical exercises will help you draw up and
interpret a horoscope, the map of the heavens that is the
basis of the astrologer's art.

Graham Boston is an experienced astrologer, both lecturing
in the subject and using it as a counselling tool. He has also
written extensively on astrology and its relevance to career
choices.

A BEGINNER'S GUIDE

PAGANISM

Teresa Moorey

paganism is the worship of Nature. It does not involve lists of rules or dogmas – it concentrates on the celebration of life itself.

This lively introduction describes the practices and basis of paganism by considering the following:

- the honour of the Goddess figure
- witchcraft and wicca; cycles and celebrations
- shamanism; druidry; Celtic paganism
- the Northern Tradition; feminism
- the men's movement
- eco-pagans and cyber-pagans

Although there are many different forms of paganism, *Pagnism – A Beginner's Guide* outlines the underlying worship and gives a clear and concise guide to inform and inspire!

A BEGINNER'S GUIDE

shamanism

Teresa Moorey

Follow the path of shamism to discover self-knowledge and kinship with all beings – plants, animals, and the Earth herself. Shamanism is more than a New Age pastime; it is a way of being that is open to anyone who seeks it sincerely.

- Expand your perceptions beyond the everyday.
- Experience shamanic journeying.
- Learn from the wisdom of the medicine wheel.
- Discover your power animal and how it can help you.

Simple exercises put your newly acquainted knowledge into practice.

Teresa Moorey is a qualified practising counsellor and astrologer and has followed the path of witchcraft and goddess worship for most of her adult life. She has written extensively on nature worship and astrology.